Rive gauche
Rive droite

MARC JANCOU (ED.)

jrp|ringier

Table of Contents

A Sesame for Paris

Alexis Jakubowicz

It would be nice to really get into Paris for the first time, and never get over it. Leave my hotel room at about nine in the morning and breakfast on a range of clichés. Have my first croissant and first *café crème* before lunch, then a ham baguette and a bottle of Vittel mineral water. In the evening, I'd order six *escargots* on the rue de Buci but only eat three. I'd drink Brouilly and walk down to the Pont des Arts along the side-streets, off the main stage of the rue de Seine. I'd take the back streets from Saint-Germain-des-Prés and cross the cobblestones of the Institut de France, stepping through the night in the cool shadow of the scholars. Finally, I would fall asleep—without shutters, without remorse—in the dirty light of the street lamps, tired and happy from conquering new territories. I want Paris to make me ache with effort; I want its life to give me migraines and its exhaustiveness to tire me out! I wouldn't go and sit in the double-decker coaches where tourists, copied and pasted to their iPhones, click away at the

Louvre, voiding their batteries and their memories. Weariness is the entropy of time, the poetics of space, and each visitor must test the mettle of their task in it.

In an age of interconnectedness, major exhibitions now resemble the cities that host them. They are like public transport networks. Over the course of the day, they sweep along thousands of rubberneckers accustomed to taking the metro and using in-car navigation systems or museum audio-guides. "Turn right," "take the next left, get out, get in," "look: you have arrived at your destination." Alas, distance is no longer a necessity of experience, and thanks to the omnipotence of Google, we can all travel *à la carte*. Why keep your feet on the ground when you can spy on the whole universe from the comfort of your own sitting room? Martin Heidegger raised this question in a different context: "In *Dasein* there lies an essential tendency toward closeness,"[1] as he wrote in 1927. He later acknowledged (in 1950) that television represented "the peak of this abolition of every possibility of remoteness."[2] In short, the cybernetic moment, born at the dawn of the 1950s in the United States, shrank the world, and, correlatively, imagination.

These days, *Homo informaticus* moves between street and museum, following cultural events like applications on a smartphone. He makes sure to *receive* information before *perceiving* the presence of works of art. He exerts neither his body nor his mind, losing his sense of direction and abstaining from tropism, intuition, and digression—the energy of pleasure. Jean-François Lyotard draws on this *absence of distance* to conclude the existence of a fundamental aesthetic problem of the medium and site of inscription:

> The futility of all iconographic, iconological, semiological, sociological, and psychoanalytic methods that do not begin by precisely establishing the position of the plastic elements—line, value, color—in relationship to the screen. The specificity of meaning resides in this position alone. It is absurd to apply the same categories to the Ravenna mosaics and Magritte's paintings. What is crucial is the nature of the site of inscription. This nature is always in an understandable relationship with the position of society in relation to itself.[3]

While museums vie to outdo each other in terms of digital marketing, art is removed from the physical dimension, tipping over into a world of networks, which, as we can see, distorts the plurality of sites of inscription in favor of the screen. Websites, interactive floor plans, and virtual tours all serve as anti-phenomenological mediators that are incompatible with the notion of plasticity, which Catherine Malabou defined with reference to Hegel as "the achievement of presence and its deflagration, its emergence and its explosion."[4]

The 21st century's media potential represents a challenge to this widely accepted state of affairs and refuses to allow the artist to pursue the task assigned to him by Paul Klee: the artist "neither serves nor rules—he transmits."[5] Modern, and now contemporary, art have found a marvelous solution for disseminating form in history. Like the works of Robert Ryman, whose wall attachments extend beyond the work itself,[6] artists have shown how to "shift the gaze from the center of the work to the edges, then the periphery: its staging in space."[7]

Yet the age of the television established a particular way for events to appear through non-events, which incites us to "forget the exhibition." In bringing technological mediation into general use, museums imitate the conditions of the *hic et nunc*, transporting aesthetic experiences as if they were information, everywhere and nowhere rather than *here* and *now*.

It has become crucial to recreate the notions of distance and time necessary to experience art. Marc Jancou's exhibition is an auspicious attempt to re-establish the contemporary audience's most fundamental rights—to think, be aware, be moved, and to tire. The explosion of presence is radical, but plasticity is resolved in six sites, intimately positioned in reality. I see here an apt response to the doubts expressed by William Rubin in 1970:

> Museums never were, and I think never will be, the absolutely right environment for works of art. I don't think works of art are at their most interesting when separated from the whole fabric of life. It makes it possible for more of the public to see them, it's convenient, it's good for art history—especially as it preserves them—but it is a compromise.[8]

What makes *Rive gauche/Rive droite* different is its outright refusal to compromise. Here, art is not decontextualized as it would be in a museum, to meet the expectations of some curator; nor is it denatured by political motivations, as is the case for public art. The exhibition replaces the white cube, devoid of past, present, and future, with spaces inhabited *a priori* by souls and objects. The works are taken down from their pedestals and their original meaning is maintained as they are delicately fitted into the spaces that host them. Each part of the exhibition is far enough removed from the others to require an effort, without disrupting the viewer's concentration. Art becomes an *in vivo* stroll, a pleasure as delightful as a certain Parisian lifestyle.

Museum visits are always subject to the institutional imperatives of silence, educational reading, and curatorial organization—in a word, Culture. Unlike a museum, *Rive gauche/Rive droite* calls on the streets of Paris to direct the one-way flow of the visit. The positive experience of art is rendered "negative" by the alternation of low-key moments *outside* the exhibition in a space full of life. The visitor thus becomes an outsider—an absent-minded stroller who interrupts his walk to admire displays in shop windows, stop at sidewalk cafés along the way, or read some pages of the present catalogue amid the hubbub of a city square.

The present book is a moveable feast, a mobile object for the meanwhile, an aid to the counter-visit. It is an antidote to the bedazzlement we experience when our retinas, surreptitiously saturated by works of art, demand the attention of reason. Read *Rive gauche/Rive droite* along the way, to tire your mind. Between sites, the art works its way under the visitors' skin and into their muscles; they judge it within their bodies. Such soma-aesthetics are the very marrow of this catalogue, whose format is designed for visitors to take it along. Each page turned is a step; the book as a whole is choreography for the mind.

No matter if you stay in each exhibition space for two minutes or two hours—art is a comet, an anecdote whose light is a memory, and memory a judgment. This catalogue is designed to withstand movement and has to travel over a distance to increase in efficiency. Take it on its paces through the streets of Paris, keep it in your pocket like a magic key, blend in with the crowds, hide your presence in the lives of others. No one will know that you are an incognito visitor in a museum—and if, by chance, some do hold your gaze, you should ask yourself whether they might not be an unnamed accomplice.

NOTES

1 Martin Heidegger, *Being and Time*, trans.
   J.M. Macquarrie and E. Robinson, Blackwell, Oxford
   1962, p. 140.
2 Martin Heidegger, "The Thing," in *Poetry, Language,
   Thought*, trans. Albert Hofstadter, Harper and Row,
   New York 1971, p. 165.
3 This footnote (208) is at the end of the central chapter
   in Lyotard's *Discours, Figure* (Klincksieck, Paris 1971).
   The chapter is entitled "Veduta sur un fragment de
   l'"histoire' du désir." Quoted in Jean-Louis Déotte,
   "Lyotard : la thermodynamique des appareils,"
   in *L'époque des Appareils*, Lignes & Manifestes,
   Paris 2004, p. 82.
4 Catherine Malabou, *Plasticity at the Dusk of Writing:
   Dialectic, Destruction, Deconstruction*, trans.
   C. Sheard, Columbia University Press, New York 2009,
   p. 8.
5 Paul Klee, *On Modern Art*, trans. Paul Findlay,
   Faber and Faber, London 1966, p. 11.
6 I am thinking here particularly of the *Untitled* series
   (1980–2003).
7 Pierre Leguillon, "Oublier l'exposition avec un luxe
   de details," in *Art Press*, special issue 21, *Oublier
   l'exposition*, 2000, p. 12–14.
8 William Rubin, quoted in Lawrence Alloway and
   John Coplans, "Talking with Rubin," *Artforum* XII,
   no. 2 (October 1970), p. 53.

The Ice-Cream Seller
at the Eiffel Tower

Yves Aupetitallot

A few years ago—in 1993, to be precise—Marc Jancou came up with the idea for an exhibition in La Bocca, the restaurant that replaced the famous Bistrot des Halles on rue Montmartre (in Paris, as if it needed saying ...). He showed the work of a score of artists and published a book to which I, along with others, was invited to contribute a text.

The roots of that exhibition and book lie in the ideas that Marc set forth in his preface: something along the lines of decontextualizing the way art is presented by moving toward a functional space with powerful connotations, in the shape of a site associated with gourmandise. This, he wrote, would set the scene for a paradoxical societal recontextualization of art.

Between the two polarities of his argument there arose questions of time, of a new art cuisine, most of whose experiments and sedimentations have since evaporated, or, more prosaically, have been unceremoniously digested.

Marc Jancou has now returned to Paris to serve up another helping of an ever-unfinished ritual of art of the moment, developing it in six spaces across Paris, half-way between public art and domestic interiors—sites that can be described as "intermediary" in a city that has been endowed with a profusion of institutions devoted to contemporary art over the past few decades.

The situation has changed since 1993, but the question of the site where art is presented, particularly on the French, particularly Parisian, scene, remains one of the key issues in Marc Jancou's curatorial work. In this he remains very close to the prevailing critical discourse of the 1960s and 1970s, which seems to form the backdrop to his formative years in art, or at least to have influenced him considerably.

The site of art and the ways in which works are produced, collected, and displayed have much to tell us about the status of art and its dialectical relationship with its milieu, whether social, political, or otherwise.

In this context, Marc Jancou has made an explicit statement by choosing sites across Paris that lie outside the institutional field; he is aware of the paradox of a country that constantly monitors the universality of its culture and the appeal of its cultural output.

Greatness has been a constant theme ever since André Malraux made his speech at the inauguration of the Maison de la Culture in Bourges in 1964: "Some countries are never greater than when they are great for others. France is not inward-looking. For the whole world, France means the Crusades and the Revolution. The tombs of French knights and revolutionaries lie along all the great routes of Europe. Rethinking the identity of our nation means being for others what we have borne within ourselves. We must bring together the greatest number of artworks for the greatest number of people."

At the same time, as non-Communist Europe was beginning to build art centers, Kunsthallen, and museums devoted to contemporary art as part of a movement that was to grow exponentially over the following two decades, France focused on its cultural exception, building Maisons de la Culture that reflected the national resolve to encourage social cohesion. These buildings were signs of the supposed collective engagement with culture and became key sites in sharing the ontological foundations of a national community keen to define its identity, its modernity, and its social cohesion in one interwoven movement. The key cultural form of this shared experience was the theater, both as space and as text, presenting its language to an auditorium filled with a cross-section of a society smelted in the educational forges of non-denominational schools, preserving the French language as a common cultural heritage. It can easily be seen how art that echoes the individual visitor's self-regarding contemplation gave rise to a certain degree of mistrust. Its most excessive expression dismissed such art as mere bourgeois entertainment and speculative trade. It owes its rehabilitation in recent years to considerable efforts at mediation for the educational community and groups of schoolchildren.

Art became part of the consensus of knowledge and the transformation of reality through culture once it worked out how to create ways to bring communities together in common communion.

The phenomenon observed by Tino Sehgal at the Musée des Beaux-Arts in Nantes underpins his 2007 work, *This Success or This Failure*, which has been shown at the ICA in London, in Bregenz, and at the MAGASIN in Grenoble. Classes of schoolchildren take over an empty exhibition space and ask each visitor if the exhibition is a success or a failure.

The situation developed in France in the early 1980s as a combined result of a financially generous cultural policy, and the mistrust aroused by those in charge of implementing it, who had been vocal in their radical critique of the avant-garde. Pierre Gaudibert was particularly incisive: "These trends ran out of steam in the 1970s [...] at the same time, there was a reflexive retrenchment, a bulimia of theorization, a tedious repetitiveness in both analysis and craft, and a proliferation of modernist forms of academicism. Intellectualist avant-gardes pushed their way to the front of the stage ... "

The artists in the circle around Buren, Sarkis, and many others reacted against this by striving to create alternative spaces to bring together, juxtapose, connect, and demonstrate the alterity of their positions.

The renowned collector Bob Calle, who was also director of the Institut Curie, placed a church facing demolition at their disposal in 1981. Like Seth Siegelaub's exhibitions, our two artists, together with Jean-Hubert Martin, Michel Claura, and Selman Selvi, planned an exhibition as a "work in progress," with no set dates and with constantly redefined outlines. They regularly extended invitations to networks of French, German, and American artists accustomed to showing their work at biennials and Documentas. Among them was Dan Graham, who summed up the undertaking thus: "It made me think of the New York alternative space in the 1970s. The first such space in New York was at 112 Green Street, founded by Matta-Clark and Jeff Lew ... The exhibition represented a freer, less bureaucratic and centralized way of approaching art, adopted at the time by the new Socialist government. It represented the new, pure national content, based on the French language, which the government also was also keen to promote."

The same drive to provide alternative spaces was behind other experiments, particularly in the provinces. The CAPC in Bordeaux and the MAGASIN in Grenoble took over industrial wastelands, carrying out a basic redevelopment of the site and using the central space—the central hall in the case of Bordeaux and the "street" in the case of Grenoble—to create monumental works in situ. It is worth noting— and this will be my concluding remark—that the Parisian scene has been dominated in recent years by two major initiatives in terms of space, the Palais de Tokyo and Monumenta, which is held in the hall of the Grand Palais. Both clearly derive their initial intellectual impetus from the aforementioned experiments in the provinces, but give an academic coloring to the constitutive original elements, at a time when curatorial practice and the spaces of all kinds which host them have migrated toward other typologies and topologies.

Marc Jancou's *Rive gauche/Rive droite*, like his *Restaurant*, shows all the appeal of this Parisian scene—and its limits.

Alexandra Bircken, *Icarus Survivor*, 2009 →

Alexandra Bircken, *Containerland*, 2009 →→→

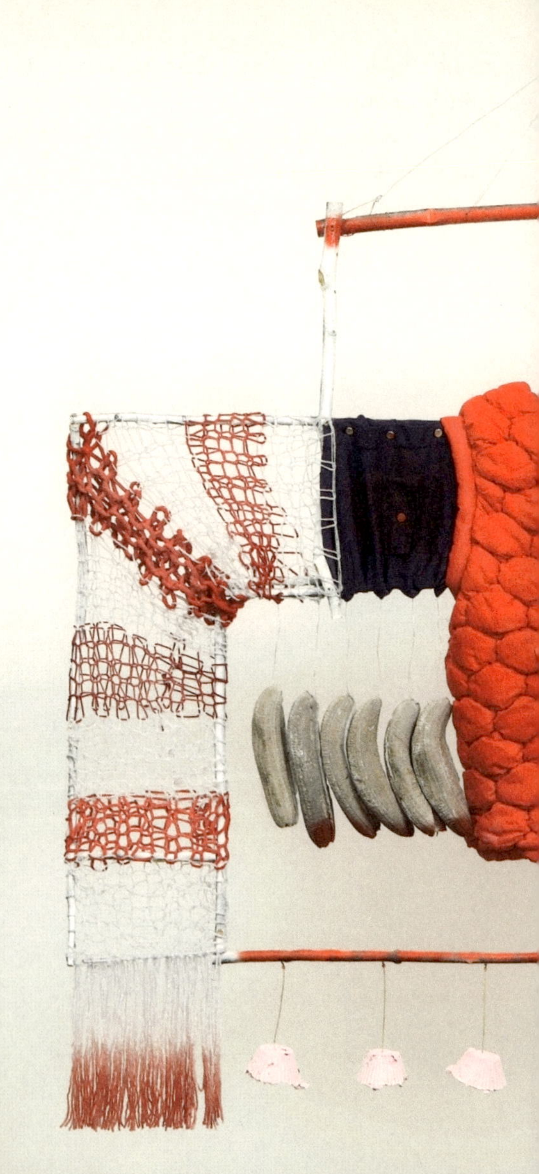

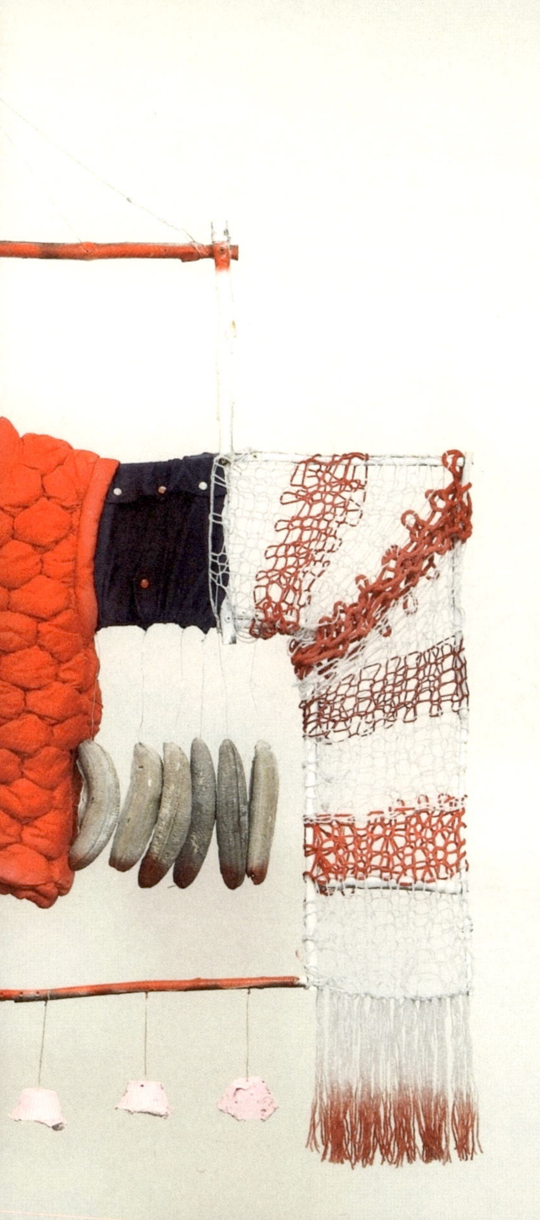

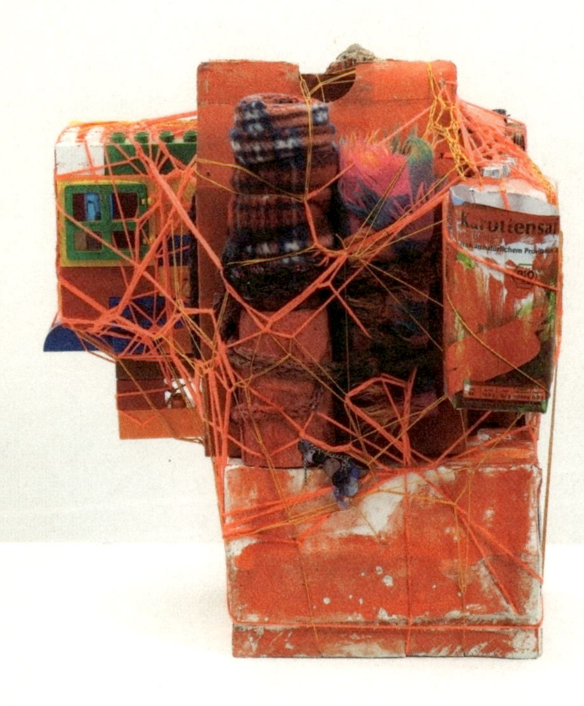
Karottensaft
naturlichem Produkt

Questionnaire

Marc Jancou and Lionel Bovier

What are the cultural and artistic references in your work? What are you currently reading, looking at, and listening to?

STEVEN CLAYDON: The nature of the work is that it is culturally very absorbent, spongy, porous. It sucks in and spits out. Old stuff and new. WOW. That's not my doing. It's against my wishes mostly. The best you can hope of a work is that it behaves like a gaping reflection bedecked with lures like a deep-sea fish. I just finished *Guignol's Band* by Louis Ferdinand Destouches Céline and some Flann O'Brian books. WFMU.

JIM SHAW: Currently investigating the perversities and accidental mysticism of silver-age Superman, investigating William Blake, Carl Jung, Rudolf Steiner, Led Zeppelin, Francis Bacon, Max Ernst, right-wing Christianity, listening to psychotic Christian kids' records, compilations of 78s from all over—the usual psychedelic stuff.

MICHAEL BAUER: Mavi Isiklar: Ain't that so // The Wickerman: OST // The Fall: Afro Ibis Man // Parasites of the Western World: Mo // Bobby Soxx: Hate in the 80s // Braque: Jeanette // Ghedalia: Tazartes // Mike Wilhel: Junko Partner // Gandalf: Can You Travel In the Dark Alone // Toncho Pilatos: Dejenla en paz // Tom Russel Band: Downtown Train // Bachdenkel: An Appointment with the Master // State Children: Control Mama // Willie Nelson: How Long Is Forever // Iron Knowledge: Showstopper // Boyd Rice + Frank Tovey: Extraction 2 // Master Musicians of Bukakke: People of Drifting Houses // Wendy Rene: Bar-B-Q // Jungle Jim: Big Fat Oranguman // Ballistic Kisses: Whose Mama Is This // Clipse: Dirty Money // Blair Petrie: Restaurant // Sheena Easton: For Your Eyes Only // Omar Soueyman: Shift Al Mani // Craig Leon: Donkeys Bearing Cups // Keith Cross and Peter Ross: The Dead Salute // Empirial Sleeping Consort: Dream Side I // Deep Jew: Master // Bacteria: Facce grigie // Mavi Isiklar: Kanamam // Stark Reality: Junkmans Song // Ike Reiko: Kokotsu no seka (LP) // AMM + Merzbow: For Ute // Chuck and Mac: Powerful Love

ALEXANDRA BIRCKEN: *Cacti and Succulents: Step-by-Step Guide to Growing Success.*

CHRISTIAN HOLSTAD: I'm interested in where the crossroads of New Age philosophy and modern consumerism meet. I'm also interested in all forms of self-help, and how to revitalize it. I'm reading books on Peruvian textiles and Bugatti furniture and listening to minimal house music. I'm currently in the middle of construction in my apartment, so I'm looking at a pile of garbage.

CARTER: Truman Capote: *Conversations*; *The Six Schizophrenias. A Clinical Study*, published in 1954 (I like reading outdated material); *The Perfect Medium, Photography and the Occult*; *House and Gardens Complete Guide to Interior Decorating*, 1958; *Flowers: Their Arrangement*, 1940 (flowers arranged in 1940 are much differ-ent than contemporary flower arrangements). These are homosexual readings, which are much different than heterosexual readings.

ROSS CHISHOLM: Over the last few years I've been looking at and using 18th-century painting, more specifically, the British society portraiture of people such as Gainsborough, Romney, and Reynolds. Although, recently, perhaps in a timely fashion, I've also been looking more at Fragonard and other old masters. Also, found cultural arti-facts such as slides and old familial Super-8 footage fascinate me, mostly gathered from car boot sales and flea markets.

I'm reading *Painting for Money: The Visual Arts and the Public Sphere in Eighteenth-Century England* by David Solkin, as well as attempting Lefebvre and Canguilhelm. Borges' *Fictions* holds a special interest for me, especially "Pierre Ménard, Author of the Quixote." W.G. Sebald and Alan Moore are writers I admire. I'm listening to Alva Noto, Acid Mothers Temple, Gallon Drunk, while looking at the Sloane Museum in London, Russian Art, Kippenberger, as well as Blake's prints for *Songs* and *Book of Job.*

MICHAEL CLINE: In the studio, over lunch, I've been reading and rereading Reader's Digest *Into the Unknown* and a few volumes devoted to the art of children. Also I've been simultaneously reading books on Max Beckmann, Thomas Hart Benton, and Stanley Spencer.

And some things that are important to me are: American Regionalism, Neue Sachlichkeit, Social Realism, Kitchen Sink Realism, and Zap Comics. I'm interested in the all the untidy loose ends and wrong turns that skulk about in the shadow of the official canon of Modern Art.

And a recap of some things I am listening to: *KEXP John in the Morning* (radio show out of Seattle), The Clientele, Deltron 3030, M83,

Tubeway Army, Swervedriver, and the Besnard Lakes.

SLAWOMIR ELSNER: Currently I am reading Fabrizio Gatti's *Bilal*—a description of the odyssey of illegal immigrants to Europe.

ANDREAS HOFER: References: .... (unlimited life of pictures as ghosts, aliens, messengers from a different time, signs, heroes, talking animals, creatures of a new dimension, stars, friends, secret beauties, miracles of love, inventors and invaders, monsters, bones of the monsters, shadows of the bones of the monsters, signals of the shadows of the bones of the monsters ...)
I am reading J.G. Ballard (*Concrete Island*), watching Robert Smithson's film about the *Spiral Jetty* and listening to ....

DES HUGHES: *The Day of the Triffids*, *The Shape of Time* by George Kubler, medieval sculpture, tomb effigies, portmanteau horror films (particularly Amicus and Hammer), any films that involve zombies or the undead.

MEREDITH JAMES: I started using passages in books as starting points for artworks. I look for visual problems that can be articulated in words but cannot exist in the real world, and I try to translate that written thought into a visual experience. The piece for this show, for instance, is based on a passage from *The Invention of Morel*, a science-fiction novel about an island inhabited by tactile projections of people from a party filmed years earlier.

JUSTIN LIEBERMAN: I guess references take a few forms in my work. The work is full of images, and these are mostly really accessible. My friend told me recently that she thought my work dealt with the *popular*. I agree. There is an aspect of my work though in which, to me, the references seem interchangeable sometimes. As though it doesn't make much difference what the images are of. That is not the work's content. You have to look a bit deeper for that than references. But there are a lot of other things I use constantly that inform the work's structures, and those may be influences. The linguistic games of Raymond Roussel, the reactionary theatrics of Picabia, and the expanding frames of Marcel Broodthaers.

I like the band Killdozer. I like Les Rallizes De Nudes. My friends send me videos. I recently read a book called *The Parallax View* by Slavoj Žižek. Now I am reading a book of essays by the artist Jimmie Durham. These contain useful ideas. I read a lot of comic books. I watch Stephen King's made-for-TV movies over and over. I have them all on video. My favorite one is *Desperation*. I have seen it 20 times or more, but I wouldn't recommend it. An interesting thing about these movies, and his fiction as well, is how poorly he writes human interaction. It is utterly banal. Syrup. And for me personally, this brings a kind of existentialism to the violence and terror. It makes it seem more real. I doubt it has much to do with his intention, and this adds to it as well. Sometimes, advertisements make me cry, or enrage me, or depress me. Diesel Ads. Fuck those. I have been very influenced by certain attitudes and ideas of Jacques Vidal and Meredith James lately through conversation and looking at their work. Colleen Asper and C. Spencer Yeh are both incredibly perceptive and inventive artists.

STERLING RUBY: My references vary quite a bit. It's possible that I am an autobiographical artist, one that only accepts cultural and artistic influences that have some relationship to my own demeanor or attitudes; perhaps that is everyone though. This confused list includes: marginalized societies, maximum security prisons, modernist architecture, artifacts and antiquities, graffiti, the mechanisms of warfare, urban gangs, pre-op versus post-op transexuals, change.org, the Lockheed Stealth F-22 Raptor,

America's Juvenile Correction System (or the absolute lack thereof). Also, Tony Smith, Ronald Bladen, Richard Misrach's *Violent Legacies*, Cai Guo-Qiang, Los Angeles County Museum's *The Spritual In Art: Abstract Painting from 1890–1985*, Anselm Kiefer, Josh Smith, Rebecca Warren, Judy Chicago, Squeaky Fromme's embroidery, the Rodarte sisters …

I am still listening to Lil Boosie's *Superbad* album that was released last year, still waiting for Young Buck's *The Rehab* to be released.

Still re-reading David Foster Wallace's *Infinite Jest* … post-suicide, Dennis Cooper's "God Jr," Louis Kahn's *Essential Texts*, Robert Jay Lifton's *Super Power Syndrome*, Jerold Kreiman's *I Hate You, Don't Leave Me*, Robert S. Nelson and Margaret Olin's *Monuments and Memory, Made and Unmade*, and Mike Davis' *Planet of Slums: Urban Involution and the Informal Working Class* …

JACQUES VIDAL: I don't make reference to things in my work, if someone asks where a certain style or shape or color comes from, I can usually trace it for them, but typically it does not aid in the understanding of any work. I find myself titling my collages for instance after the origins of the images in them, but this is usually because there is a word-game waiting within the combination of any image and word that is much better devised than things I can come up with. There is a kind of chance operation to the things I pay attention to in culture, if it seeks me out I will receive it happily … The source materials of my work lately have come from southern-Gothic fiction, far right-wing radio, and the ants that have been falling out of my ceiling.

NICK LOWE: My favorite comic book writers are Grant Morrison, Ed Brubaker, and Matt Fraction. I am not sure if what I consume informs my work directly, but I let influences penetrate my consciousness in a very elliptical manner.

RY ROCKLEN: I'm a big fan of the radio for its news and for science programs like *Radiolab* and *Quirks and Quarks*. I like learning about stuff while mindlessly assembling my sculptures. Currently I am reading *Born on a Blue Day* by Daniel Tammet. The book is an autobiography and details the life of a man who is a high functioning autistic savant who sees numbers as shapes and can make very large calculations by envisioning the different shapes the numbers generate when they are combined.

TORSTEN SLAMA: I rely heavily on model railway catalogues, as they seem to me like encyclopedias of human-made forms throughout the modern ages. My particular references have remained rather unchanged for the last 15 years. I do not want to give further information that will later on be rated according to originality or boringness. I flatter myself to have rather special interests, and I do not want that belief to be challenged. I also think it unwise to advertize the efforts of artists, writers, and musicians, who are dead, and thus do not care for a furthering of their income or fame.

CRIS BRODAHL: I am a religious painter. Life is my Bible and soundtrack.

LUCY STEIN: Having been an expat for over five years, I have become quite obsessed with British comedies like *The Thick of it*, *Funland*, *Benidorm*, *Have I Got News for You*, and so on. I like Ivor Cutler. I like fiddling around with word play and I'm always keen on artists who do the same, Hannah Wilke and Carolee Schneeman and Marlene Dumas being prime examples. They could all have been comedy writers in another life. I like things that could be trite but manage not to be. I love malapropisms and have recently been researching for a thesis on malapropism in painting as a way of breaking through the apparently hard to break seal of postmodern self-awareness. My love of humor, however, does not stop me from being critical of how much con-temporary artists rest on it to deal with the push and pull of hubris and irrelevancy. It's fun but it's not enough.

Since last Christmas I've been reading only women authors as it hit me around then that I'd read only men for a long time. Joan Didion I read and re read, the sparseness and horror of it all is very appealing to me. She is the bravest female writer I know, spare and tough as Hemingway but she never relinquishes her femaleness, her witchiness. "I know some-thing about despair." (I'm talking pre *The Year of Magical Thinking*, when she was my age or there-abouts.) *Slouching towards Bethlehem* and *Play it as it Lays* ... Susan Sontag's *The Volcano Lover* struck a big chord recently with its sensitivity and warm heartedness toward its main charac-ters, particularly the playful and charismatic singing for her supper but morally flawed Lady Hamilton of "attitudes" fame. She is the kind of female historical figure who fascinates me with her childlike beauty, shrewd and conquering intelligence and drink problem. The muse. My entire juvenilia was made up of a non-objective exploration of this stereotype in a way.

Fear of Flying by Erica Jong is a wonderful book that gets a bad press and has taught me a lot about the danger of sloganeering. A work so literary should not only go down in the annals of history as the book that introduced the concept of the "zipless fuck." I've been reading Nancy Mitford. Her barbed English tongue has touched a nerve lately. Mary Gaitskill is a brilliant writer but I'm not so keen on people who understand everything deeply but don't have the will (or ego?) to try and make or change things and most of her characters are these kind of people so I find it all hard to love, plus it depresses me a lot, I think for sex reasons. Peggy Guggenheim's autobiography is interesting as one starts off liking her and begins to dislike her exactly when one imagines her own self-loathing kicked in, it's cleverly worked out by her. Before the watershed Christmas I was in a big love affair with D.H. Lawrence for a long time but I've had to reject him for a bit, he can be so mean. I listen to Yanka the Russian on repeat for fuzzed out flights over the freakish Atlantic. Dragostea din Tei for take off. I like to watch Gossip Girl with a nip or two of green chartreuse when I'm really stressed. I read Mira Schor when I need a bolster. When I'm at the gym I listen to Professor Robert Solomon on Nietzsche or existentialism, or Professor Kenneth Bartlett on the Renaissance. Or I listen to Hole! I look a lot at Soutine, Wyndham Lewis, Francis Bacon, Paul Nash, Alice Neel, Carroll Dunham, Nicole Eisenman, Amy Sillman, and Jakob Julian Ziowlkowski, who I think is what Deleuze was talking about when he envisaged "the future of painting" through Bacon.

Des Hughes, *Dark Aged*, 2008

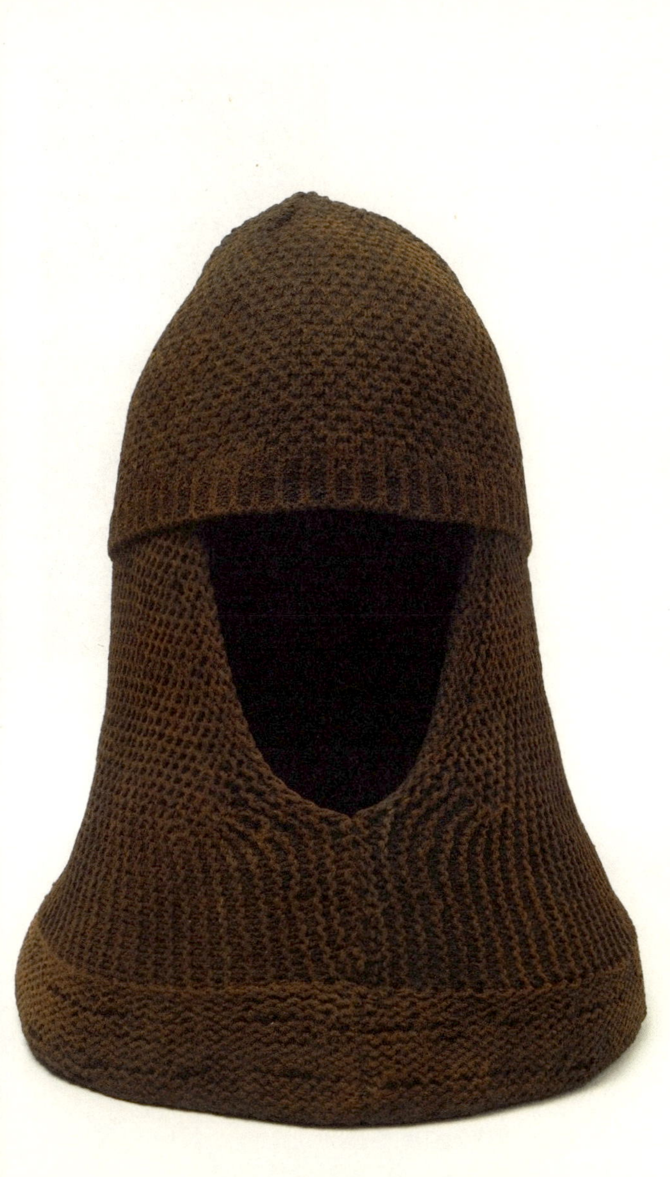

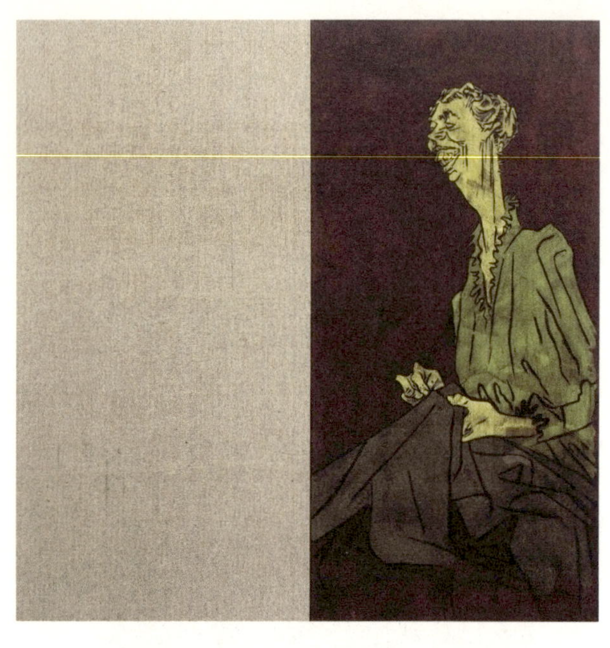

Steven Claydon, *League Diptych*, 2009

Steven Claydon, *Won from Coarseness*, 2009 →

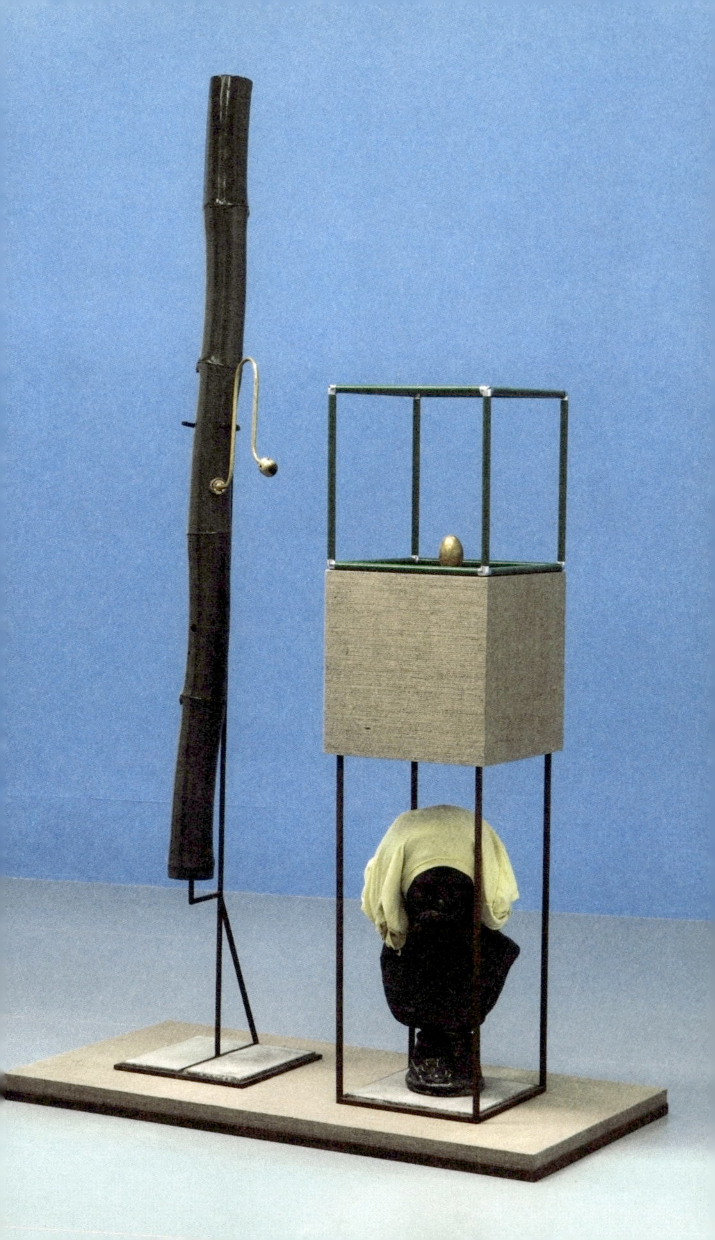

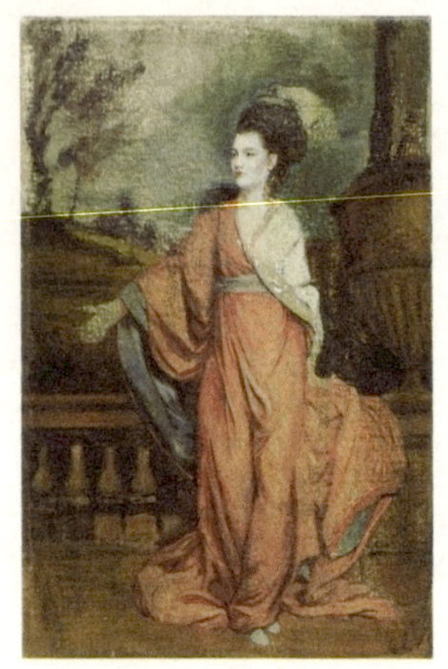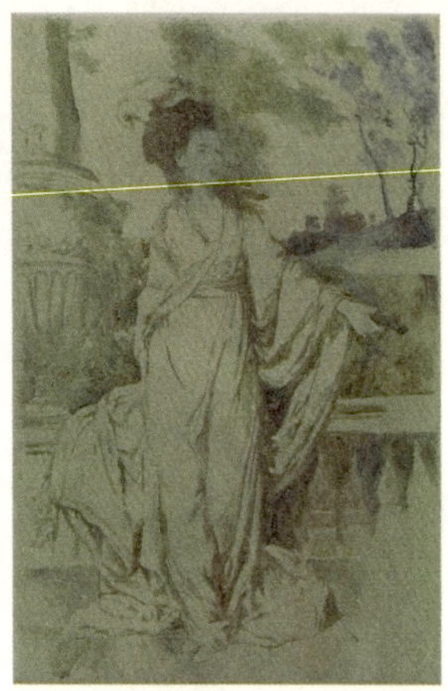

Ross Chisholm, *Urn*, 2010

40

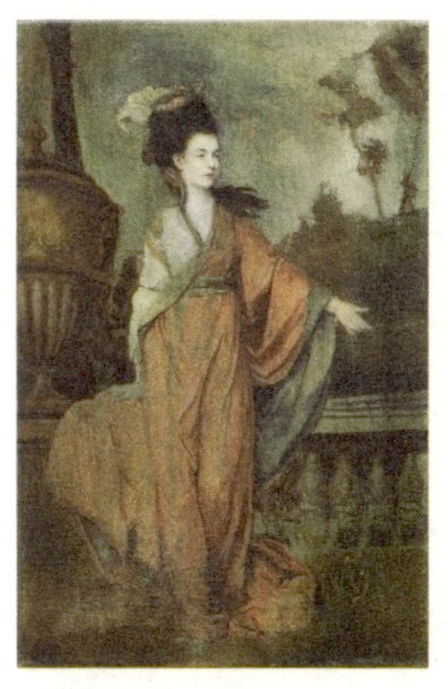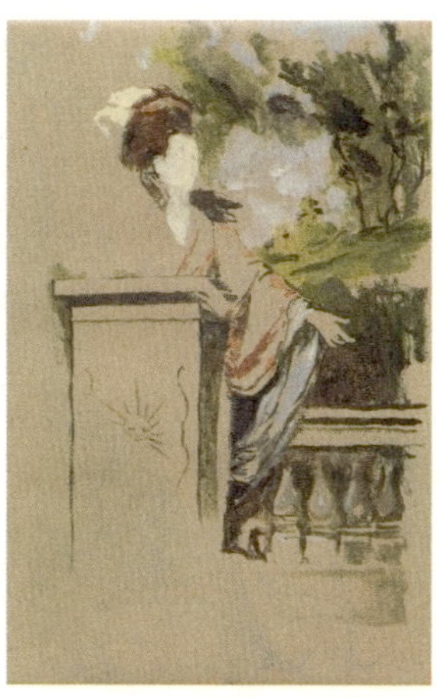

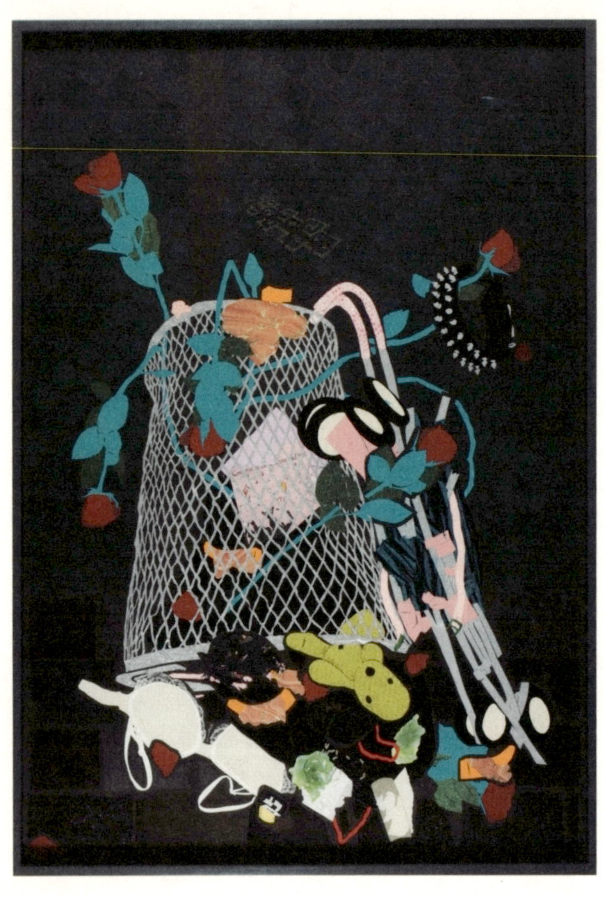

Christian Holstad, *Portrait #3 (Upside Down Can
with Prosciutto and Melon, a Bra, and an Empty Toilet
Paper Roll)*, 2009

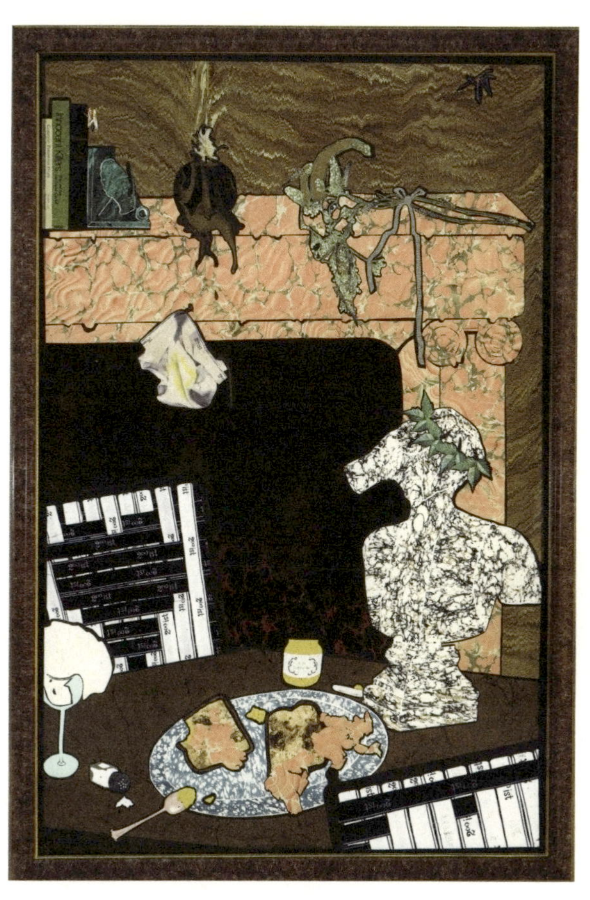

Christian Holstad, *Three Sacrifices*, 2007

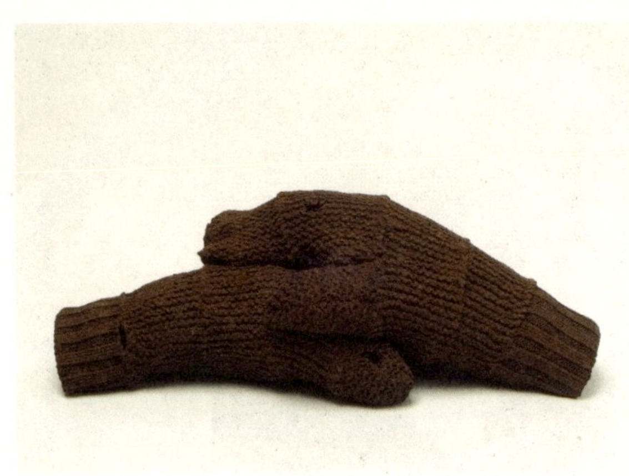

Des Hughes, *Friend of the Friendless*, 2009

To what extent does your studio practice pre-serve you from exterior contingencies? To what extent does your knowledge of current events influence your production?

JUSTIN LIEBERMAN: Not really at all. My work is pretty much staked on people's interaction with it. That is where meaning emerges. I don't think of the studio as separate from the exhibitions. Everything is always an exterior contingency. I would say that current events influence my production, but my knowledge of them much less so. My work is its own current event, and so it necessarily correlates to other events occur-ring at the same time. Like those events, it is in a state of constant reassessment and redefinition.

STEVEN CLAYDON: It appears to me that exterior contingencies have become interior. We are cooked from the inside like microwaved lumps. If I could convince this computer to leave the stu-dio, banished in auto-exile, I could return to the pastoral idle to which you refer. Current events behave like apparitions anyway; they are fleet-ing; intangible. I can only really digest exterior events and my own stupid actions through their consequences and symptomatic signs etc. So, yes, it is unavoidable sooner or later. Capice?

ALEXANDRA BIRCKEN: Up till now I have not used volcanic ash as a material.

ROSS CHISHOLM: In London, we're in the middle of an election campaign at the moment. I'm trying not to let it depress me but it's difficult. The piteous sight of the printed press hemorrhaging its relevance and influence is oddly hypnotic though. I normally find it very easy to become remote in the studio. To feel cut off. I suspect that's as much to do with the fact that people can rarely be bothered to come south of the Thames ... Ultimately I find the studio a generative site of durations, rhythms, and logics, where productive collisions occur more readily between the studio's nebulae than with those outside.

MICHAEL CLINE: When I'm in the studio, which is rather small, I've come to feel like I am in a womb of my making. The chosen nutrients for my art womb are specific and constant. Deep down, in my unconscious, I know what belongs and what needs to be synthesized for energy. Accordingly, world news and events make their way into my work through a kind of osmosis. I'll have the news on in the background to keep me company (art making is a lonely business) and things just wriggle their way in.

CHARLIE HAMMOND: My practice is continually affected by the news media, often generating the initial contents of the artworks, however it is important to recognize that through studio experimentation these initial inputs are clouded or lost. Satirical cartoons for example, can function equally well with little or no knowledge of the political landscape from which they emerge. Art that sets out to reflect and effect large global issues for me fails. I try to embrace an artwork's failure.

ANDREAS HOFER: My studio is a technically very advanced receiver for super-exterior contingencies. I am processing the current of events, the multidimensional resonance of messages from even the farthest stars or the most distant unknown poets, I am actually in contact with the radio on the ship that's sailing with the ghost of Arthur Cravan.

DES HUGHES: I think in part my practice is actually dependent on exterior contingencies. I would like to think that I have a rigorous strategy, but in fact my practice is actually driven by a continual chain of random anecdotal information that I chance upon from various sources, and that I feel I can to react to in terms of my previous work. The value of these ideas is decided when I try to translate them as material.

MEREDITH JAMES: Current events don't come into play in my work. I necessarily work alone but I don't really like being alone—making art is another way to talk to people. I like using my work as place to put things I see in the world that I'd otherwise forget.

STERLING RUBY: Allegorically, my work is a reflection of how current events are foreshadowing the coming end of all autonomy. I think that we are at a time where innate, expressive gestures are looked upon as disingenuous, but mourning the loss of expression is a new gesture in and of itself. This grief is the new sad authenticity. The idea of baggage figures highly into my work. I see the past as burden, the present as a dilemma because of that burden, and the future as an unforeseeable and frightening situation where we feel powerless and paralyzed.

CRIS BRODAHL: The studio is my church. The other world outside is a vibration, which of course, moves my work.

LUCY STEIN: Listening to the World Service for much of the day, I know a lot about the bombs in

Iraq and Pakistan but very little about local affairs in Germany or Britain. I don't get the rapes and stabbings (or X factor) but I'm in a trans global catastrophe bubble and hyper tuned in. My last two exhibitions took Susan Sontag's *The Volcano Lover* and Easyjet as their starting point/theme and opened almost concurrently in Amsterdam and Berlin on the day of the Icelandic Volcano. Everybody who came to Berlin for the *Easyjetsetters* show got stranded for a week. The question, therefore, should be "to what extent are current events influenced by Lucy's production?"

JACQUES VIDAL: I'd do whatever I could to produce a solution to the chaos of the world, or at least to produce a filter through which to see events happen with a kind of omniscient distance. I live on the top floor of an empty building, so I have a wide birth between me and even my most immediate community. The rest of the world comes down to me through the Internet, I take all of it in, all day, and it's too much in the end to worry about, if something catches my eyes I will write it down so that I can remember it. The last thing I wrote down was "McConell to Dems 'YOU SHALL NOT PASS.'" My point is: making art has never been a shield, but it has been a kind of leg up on the path to peaceful isolation.

One could say that each artist not only gener-
ates an oeuvre, but also an economy of production. How would you qualify yours?

ROSS CHISHOLM: I suppose there's an economy of
the lost and the found with the value of each
element fluctuating in relation to the reconfigu-
ration of its history, its source material, and
its multiplicity. I find that meanings tend to
regenerate and one work becomes complicit in
the making of another so the process becomes
expansive and consuming.

MICHAEL CLINE: I would like to dabble and experi-
ment in many different modes of making. But as
an artist and maker of things, I am also a prag-
matist (assuming that these two things are not
mutually exclusive). I must, as you put it, take
into consideration an "economy of production."
Within the time constraints of wearing different
hats—husband, father, artist, cook, house-
keeper, etc.—I must always calculate what can
be achieved without sacrificing and skimping.
Simply said, a work of art needs the time that it
needs to be made, no less.

That said, painting elbows its way to the
front of the line. It demands filial devotion and
time, and punishes when it is ignored.

ANDREAS HOFER: Yes, that's correct, and that's very important for me: I am extremely into economy; actually I use my powers and resources in a very economic way, you might say: the most efficient way, the least repetitive way, as directly as possible ... If there is for example an object ready to use (Duchamp called these things "readymades"), I prefer to take that instead of investing too much time and energy into producing it myself. The same goes for a picture: I don't like to "paint" it to the end—if you know what I mean. But, on the other hand, I don't hesitate to destroy the "economic laws" or disturb my intentions' "inherent necessities."

CHRISTIAN HOLSTAD: I just work; it's a job like any other.

DES HUGHES: Rather than concentrate on consistency, I'm much more interested in the emotional relationships that might exist between seemingly contradictory approaches to making. These circumstances and the things they produce seem to change regularly. I would consider an economy of production in terms of removing things until the sculpture starts to disappear.

JIM SHAW: I figured that in the unlikely chance I "made it" in art, I should spread the money around to other artists, so I had a lot of employees in the boom years, which allowed for the redistribution of lots of filthy lucre, but also made too many demands to make work they could contribute to, and put a lot of social pressure on me.

JACQUES VIDAL: I have always made products, I enjoy making products, these are the best products you could ever get, they will never break, even if they break.

LUCY STEIN: Very compulsive and prolific but everything superfluous gets culled and precious things get scarred for life.

RY ROCKLEN: My work strives to get the most out of the objects used as the basis for my sculptures. My practice is a cottage industry and I only need to empty my trashcan once a week.

TORSTEN SLAMA: Suboptimal, and I am not proud of this. Although I used to think that poor economic efficiency is what differentiates the fine arts from any other industry.

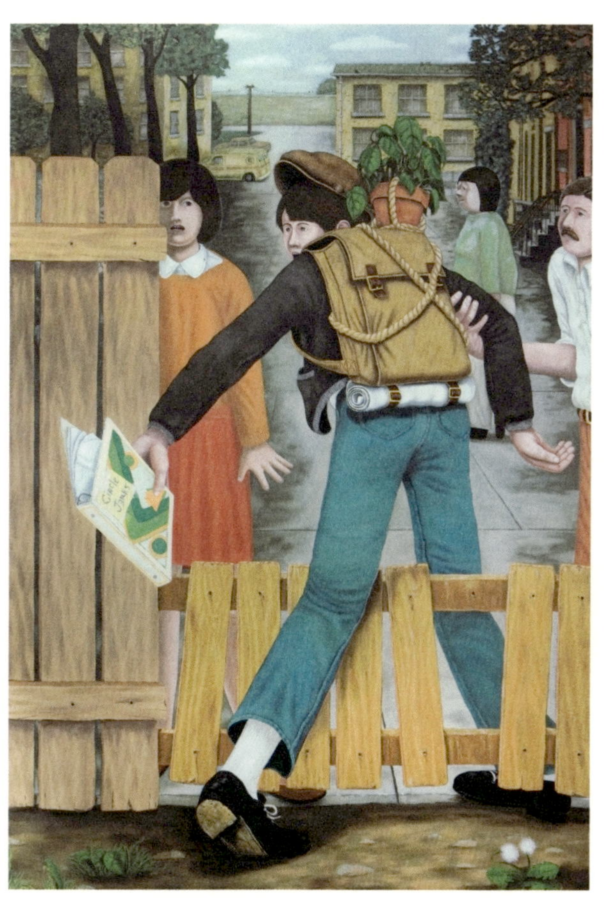

Michael Cline, *Fenced*, 2009

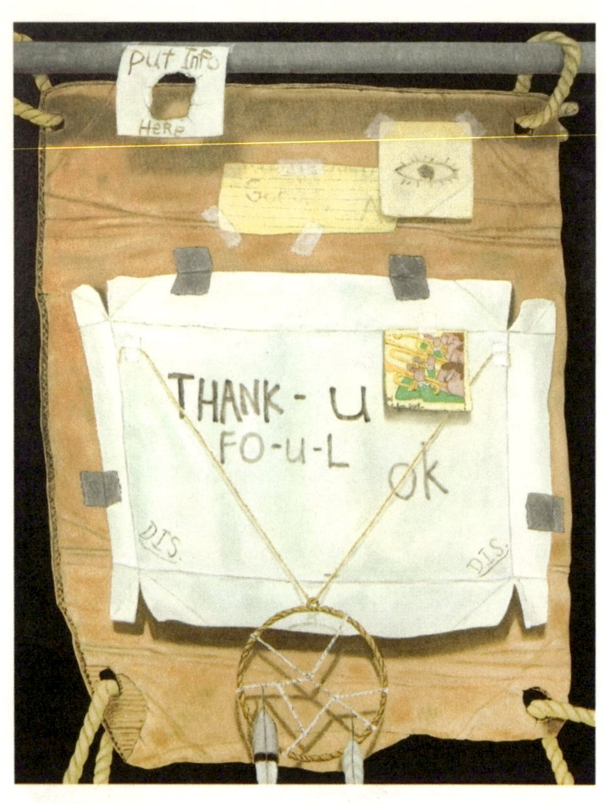

Michael Cline, *New Age Signboard*, 2009

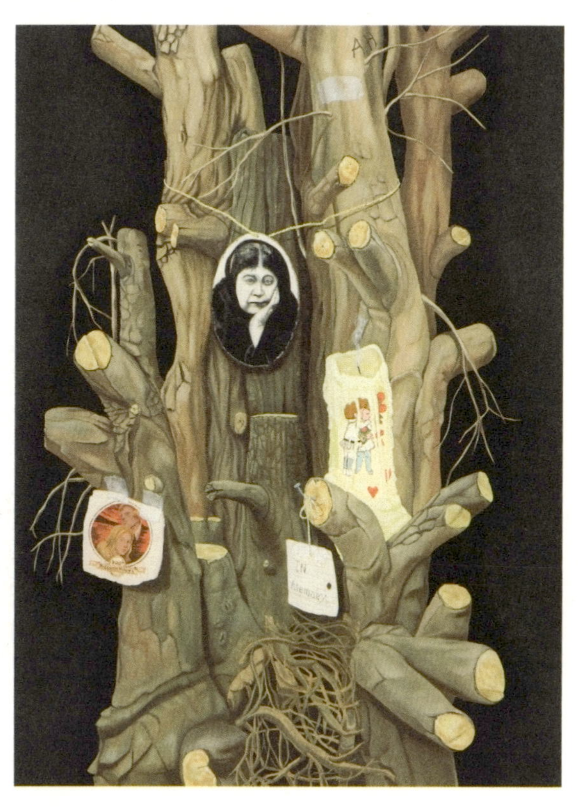

Michael Cline, *A.H.*, 2010

Justin Lieberman, *The Corrector's Custom Prefab House*, 2009 →

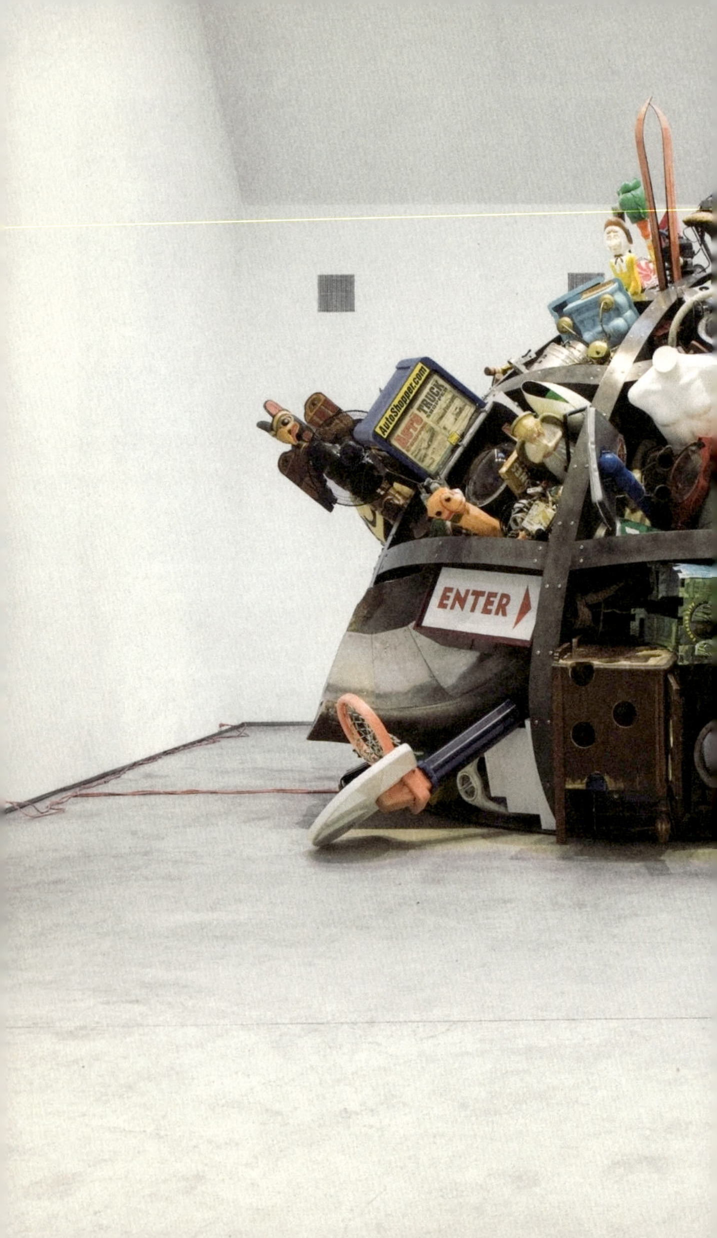

AutoShopper.com!
AUTO TRUCK
ENTER

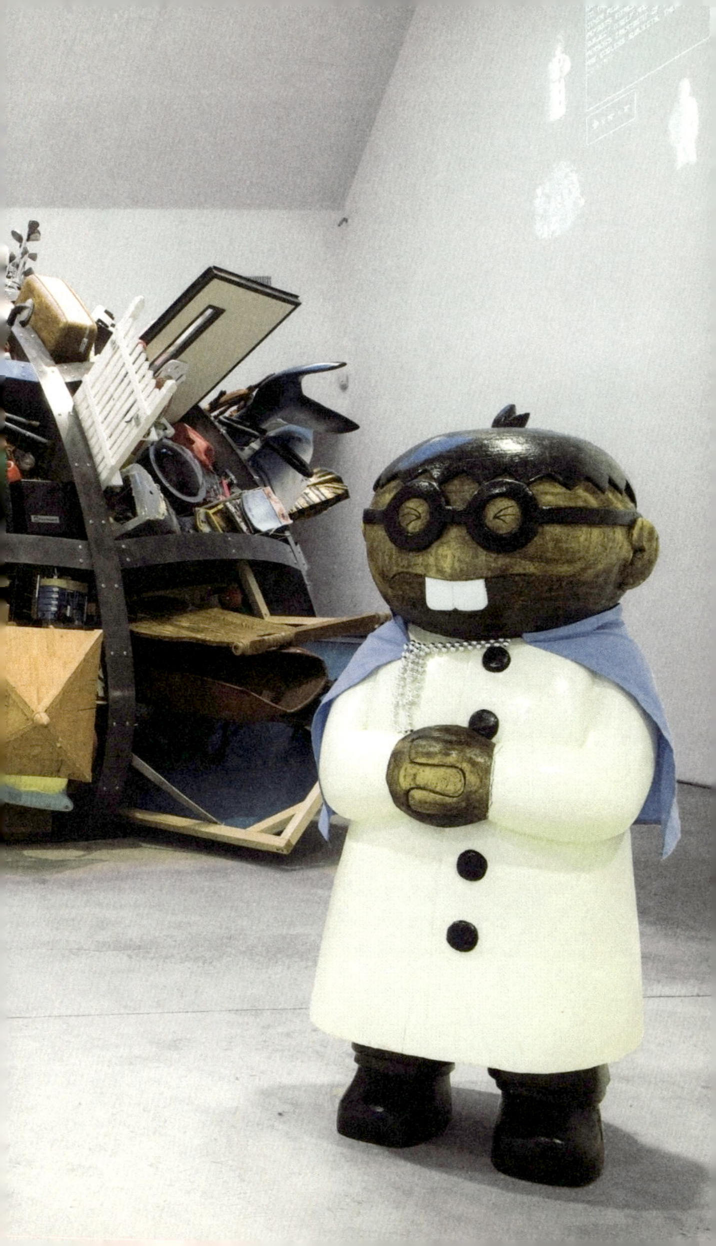

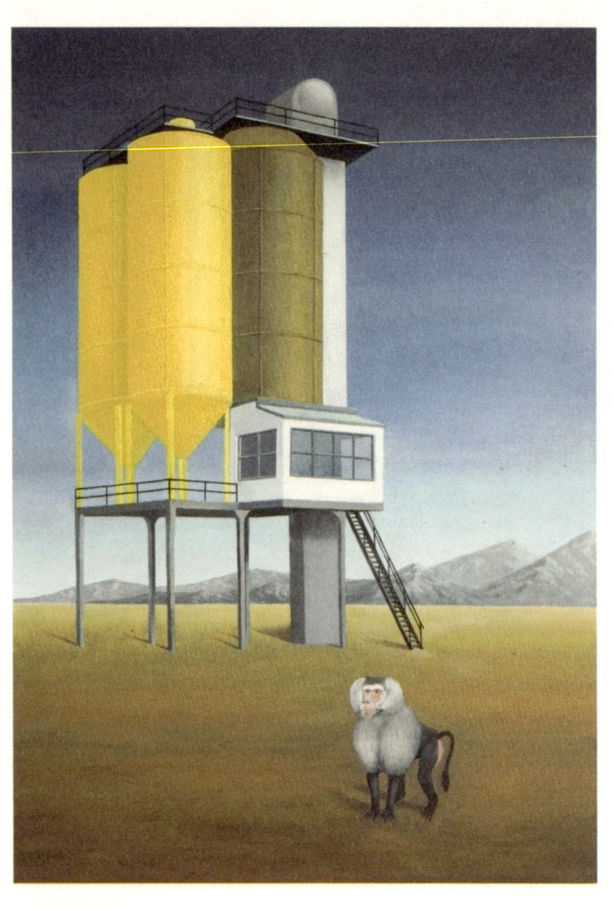

Torsten Slama, *SAPA Cement Plant*, 2008

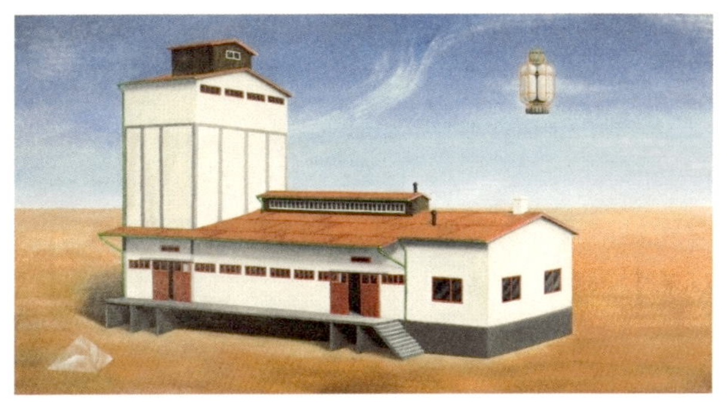

Torsten Slama, *Cooperative Raiffeisen Institute Wilhelm Reich*, 2008

Shortly after 1966, Douglas Huebler made the famous statement "The world is full of objects, more or less interesting; I do not wish to add any more." Vis-à-vis the current flow of images today, why do you feel the need to add more?

JIM SHAW: I can't help myself. Even before I had assistants, I was insanely productive. It has some elemental relationship to self-worth.

ALEXANDRA BIRCKEN: Huebler is right.

ROSS CHISHOLM: I don't feel the need not to add more. The current flow of images probably makes it easier for me to make images into things.

STEVEN CLAYDON: I think there is a certain amount of vanity in that statement, after all, humanity will excrete as long as it consumes and procreates blah blah blah. The whimsy of one voice's decent is laudable but unrealistic. Call me old fashioned. We create enough shit to drown ourselves a thousand times over. Art is just the icing on the cake.

CARTER: The Huebler comment is super depressing. I feel the need to make things because I'm alive and I'm a visual artist. I usually make things because I want to see them finished and to *have* them.

MICHAEL CLINE: Huebler is trying to be funny, right? If I'm to take it literally, it's the intellectual equivalent of holding one's breath, sooner or later you must draw air, exist, and "add more."

SLAWOMIR ELSNER: Circumstances change as time passes by. Relations between individuals as well as relations between individuals and the environment are in permanent change. It is a constant process of adaptation. It seems that continuous communication is one of the attributes of our times—an endless flow of images and data. I wonder whether we could have survived without following "the new." It is great that we are able to respond to changes and this triggers further reactions. This is "the way things go" as Peter Fischli and David Weiss have visualized so beautifully.

CHARLIE HAMMOND: If I believed that artworks remained a constant unchanging product, then perhaps they are lumps of something doing nothing; however, even if my work has a short lifespan, changing contexts have to count for something.

The biggest dilemma for a painter now is becoming simply a series of jpegs, in real terms a painting's slow production and unchanging imagery sets itself not so much in opposition to this flow imagery but as a real world encounter, maybe a short break.

ANDREAS HOFER: OK. Huebler is easy to understand but you can just as easily misunderstand him. Sure: if it's only about "adding," I don't want to "add," and if it's only about the "flow of images," I don't want to ride that wave … But is it really our problem, that there are too many images overwhelming us? I think the talk of too many images is a stupid, illogical, ideological formula, set into being by exactly the people who are producing images. It's a kind of pseudo-critique of the world of images that doesn't help, that doesn't provide a good analysis, that does not lead us to a proper use of reality, of our possibilities: I am into the secret life of the images and ourselves—the "too many" and the "adding" are not our problem; there is only inventing and giving more space to our inventions, developing, enlarging …

CHRISTIAN HOLSTAD: It isn't that there are too many things, it's that too much of it is ugly garbage.

DES HUGHES: I understand the slogan as a provocation that questions certain conditions for production that had gone before, but assume that, as a well known Conceptual artist, he would have gone on to produce numerous "works" in the form of documentation or artifacts. But a statement as an artwork still feels incredibly liberating. For me, it also suggests the problem of producing something original when a model usually already exists somewhere else in the world. I think that the best, or only way to understand something, is to attempt to remake it.

MEREDITH JAMES: I don't think of art as adding images or objects to the world, but rather as articulating ways in which to deal with existing images and objects. When I like an artwork, I imagine applying the artist's process as a filter through which I might encounter the world and deal with visual information.

NICK LOWE: Chris Hardwick, the comedian/host of G4's *Web Soup* said that we are no longer in the information age, we are in the information filtering age. There is a big pile out there, and it is now more important than ever to have artists to make poetic sense of the endless stream of images.

RY ROCKLEN: Because my practice is based on the reclamation and exaltation of found objects I am not adding any more to the world. I am simply renovating a population of objects,

TORSTEN SLAMA: To my great chagrin, I lack entrepreneurial spirit. I have a childish, or rather primitive interest in making images. (I seem to believe with a part of my brain in the magic qualities of images. Maybe I could qualify and rationalize this belief with a deeper understanding of the nature of archetypes.) I have a desire for recognition and pecuniary compensation; this constitutes my motivation to add these images to the collection of human-made objects that populate the world. My needs are of a different nature.

LUCY STEIN: Certainly I don't want to make bad or boring or even non-remarkable "images" just to illustrate my ideas. I think "the world is full of ideas, more or less interesting. I do not wish to add any more." I have more faith in my paintings, with their telltale surfaces, than my ideas.

JUSTIN LIEBERMAN: To this timely quotation, I might reply with one from Mel Bochner: "No thought can exist without a material support." Artists do not increase the number of objects in the world.

It might be the case that they reduce the number of objects by combining multiple existing objects into a single one.

STERLING RUBY: The process of adding "more" seems like an adequate way to cope with the excess; perhaps this is not a solution as much as it is a drive toward collapse.

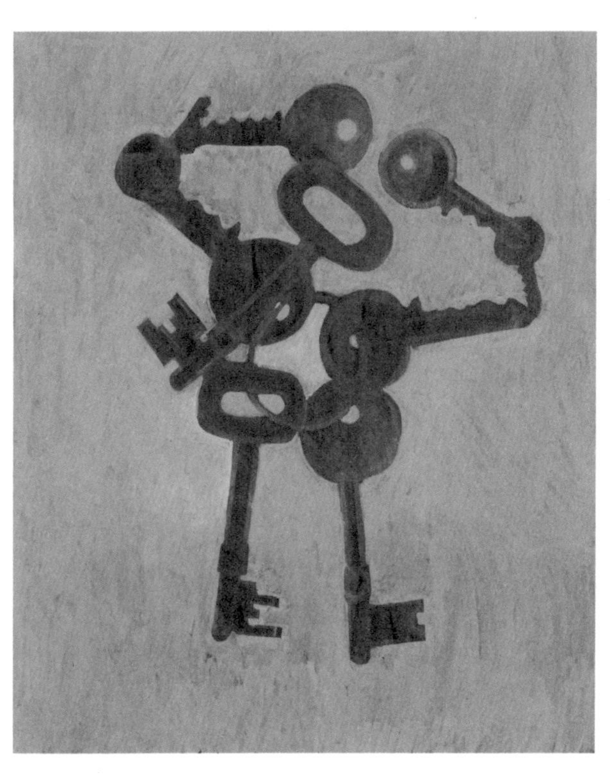

Charlie Hammond, *Portrait as a Bunch of Rusty Keys*, 2008

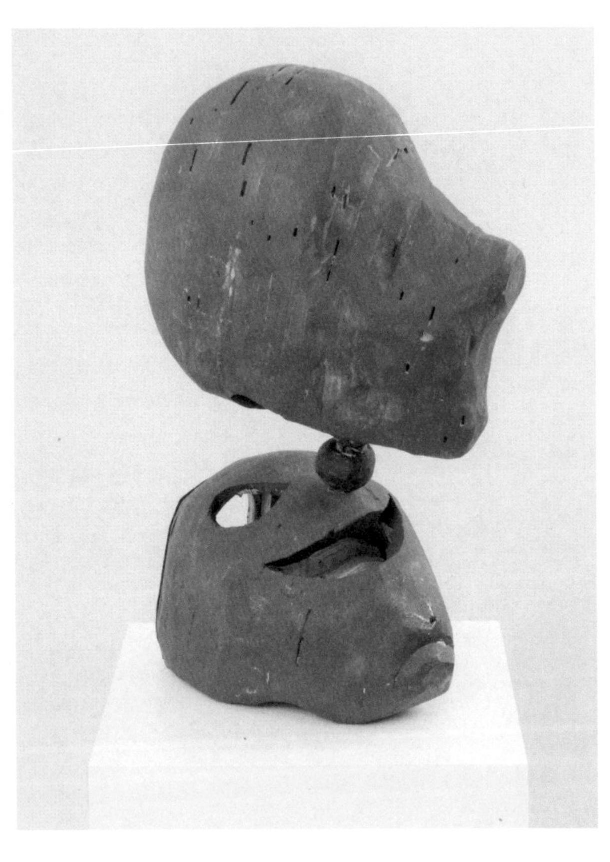

Jacques Vidal, *What-Else-Could-We-Do*, 2008

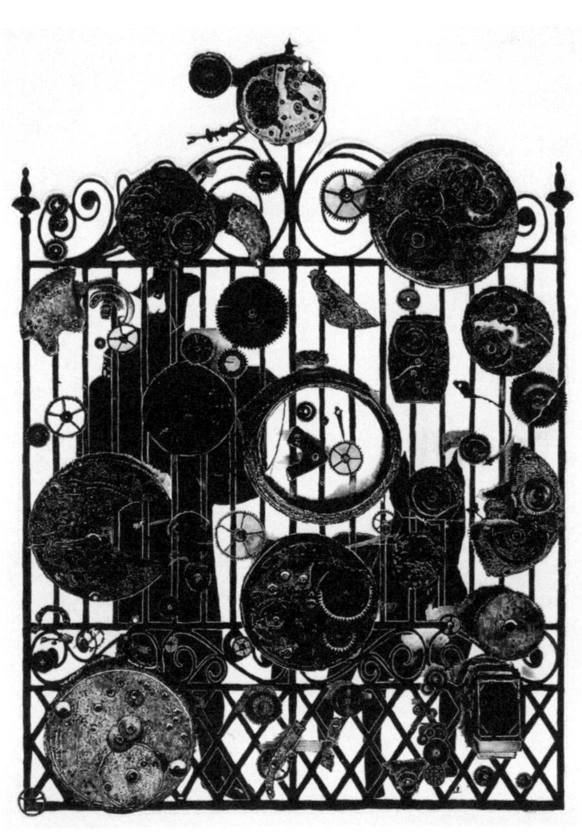

Jacques Vidal, *Guard Duty*, 2010

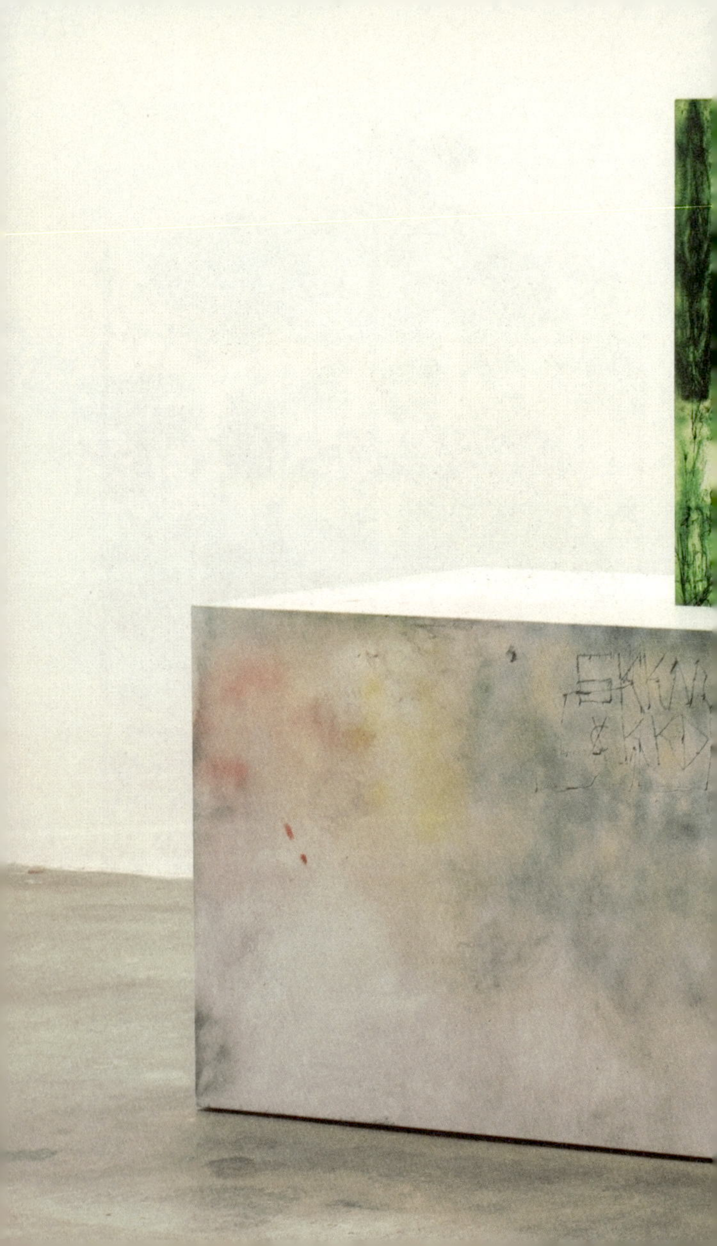

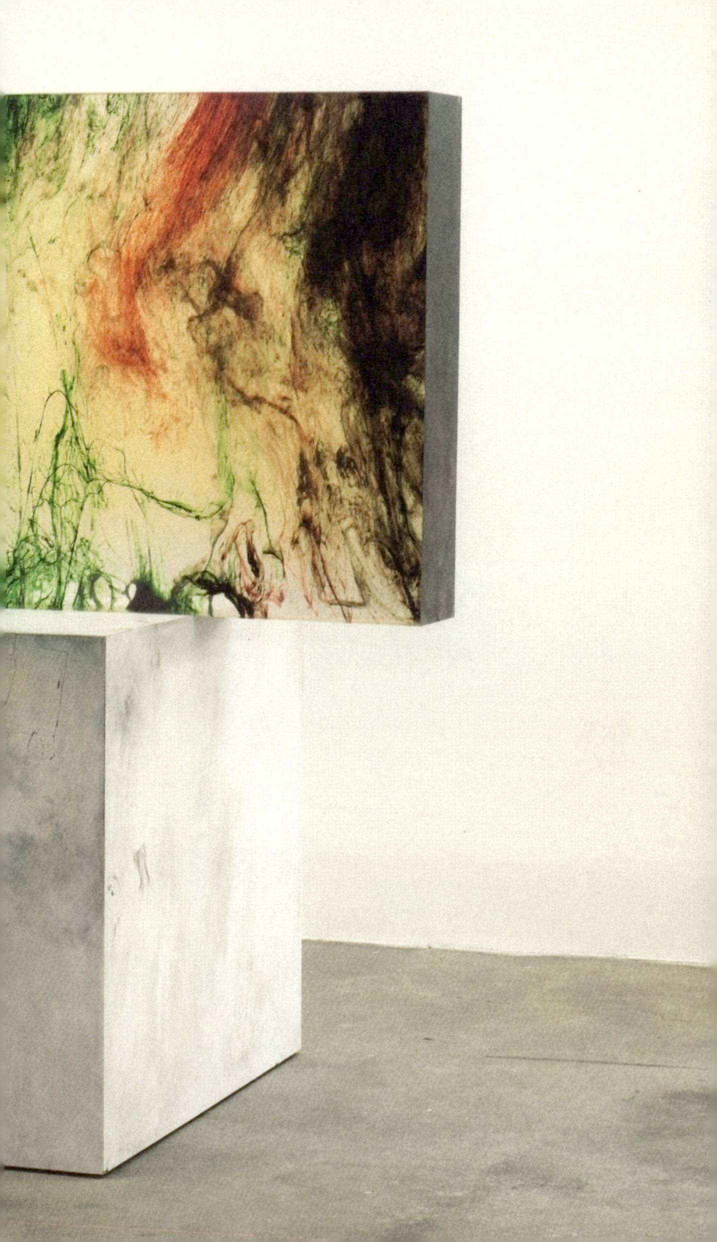

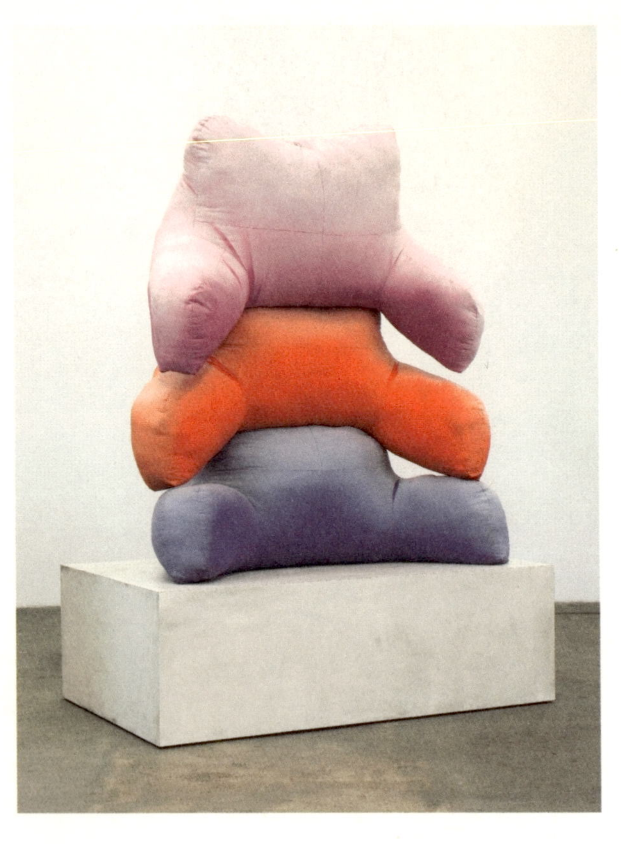

← Sterling Ruby, *ACTS/KKDETHZ*, 2009

Sterling Ruby, *Husbands/Sunburn P.O.P*, 2010

What is your relationship to the medium of painting, often considered as classical, reactionary, or flattering to the market?

STERLING RUBY: I studied painting as an undergrad in Pennsylvania, but by 1992 I stopped. I became infatuated with video art during the mid-1990s and started working at the Video Data Bank in Chicago. The Video Data Bank was started in 1968 by Kate Horsfield and Lyn Blumenthal. They saw video art as a more viable and immediate medium to create art that was political, feminist, and subjective. Kate and Lyn (and many of that time) felt that the medium was liberated by not having the history and art market value of painting; it simply did not have that baggage.

After moving to Los Angeles I started inscribing or painting these geometric sculptures. These works were very influenced by existing LA monuments that had been tagged by gangs claiming territory. I saw these pieces as conceptual. They were created in part by my reacting to theories about Minimal art's objecthood, Albert Speer's idea of "ruin value," James Quandt's "broken window theory," and general ideas of monumentality. After a few years of working this way I realized that I "was" painting, I wasn't painting on a canvas, but on a sculpture.

I felt different at this point about painting's hang-ups, I actually saw it as an opportunity to fuck with something so historically solid. I no longer felt that painting should be ignored as a statement. I bought some canvases and decided to only paint with industrial spray paint with the atmospheric aesthetics of urban graffiti, though I still thought of this as a conceptual endeavor. By the third canvas I was hooked on the activity; I started thinking about painting in terms of space, depth, punctuation, and color. I loved it. I holed up in the painting studio; it liberated me from thinking about everything needing to be defined within a conceptual, heavy-laden theoretical way of production.

STEVEN CLAYDON: As a tool I think it is a bit like Photoshop but takes longer to dry.

CARTER: I love to paint, I love classical things, and anyone who finds painting reactionary is a bore and misguided. And as far as it being "flattering to the market" ... I'm still saving up for my Hockney purchase, my Peter Saul purchase, and my Phillip Guston purchase.

ROSS CHISHOLM: We're good friends. A lot of its perceived frailties are also some of the things that make it interesting. It's quite odd to think of painting and morality in the same sentence today. A lot of the society portraits I use were not only complicit in the market, but as Solkin explains, reformulated the relationship between the market and morality. There's a weight and a texture to its multiple, mutable histories, which is fun to engage with.

MICHAEL CLINE: Painting is the foundation on which all visual art rests. I bow to it.

SLAWOMIR ELSNER: Painting is one of the oldest of all media; however, it can still be considered contemporary. As always it is the context that matters as much in painting as in any other medium.

ANDREAS HOFER: Well, as we know, art is not easy to understand and a lot of people in the institutions or in the market are "looking at art with their ears," right? Otherwise we wouldn't be bothered by the killjoy faces of Neo Rauch or the Vampire-Abstraction of Daniel Richter. But if we don't follow these well-established tendencies, the connection of painting and "classical, reactionary or flattering to the market" becomes a cliché (a kind of neoconservative left-wing *idée fixe*).

DOROTA JURCZAK: How can someone call a media reactionary? It is a neutral thing defined by its subject/contents. Classical? Reading, for instance, is also classical; playing computer games is definetly more "avant-garde," but that doesn't make reading wrong and computer games less stupid.

JUSTIN LIEBERMAN: Painting for me is a kind of beginning. The art historical thread I am most interested in has taken place largely in painting's domain. Sometimes, in dismissing work as classical, market-oriented, or reactionary, we are responding more to a work's subsumption into the very mechanisms that generate these tropes than we are to the work itself. I am always telling myself stories about how this or that thing I am making might function in the world, but these are always imaginary. I do not expect others to follow these narratives. They are for my own use. They might be a component in a larger machine that helps to drive the work, but they are not the last word. Artworks are idealistic. Often, so much so that they can seem naive. They are rarely cynical. The occupation itself almost precludes cynicism.

JIM SHAW: I enjoy it more than other mediums, but all relationships have a love/hate aspect. There is an alchemical aspect to it only similar to musical improvisation.

NICK LOWE: I love painting. I primarily make drawings, but I am always jealous of people who can channel their energy and communicate concisely through the medium of paint and brushes. My relationship to painting is like that of a beautiful woman that I want so bad and I keep making attempts to win her heart, but each time I overcome an obstacle I end up failing miserably.

TORSTEN SLAMA: If painting is classical, reactionary, and flattering to the market, I would rate these as three good reasons to paint.

CHRISTIAN HOLSTAD: I chose a semi-gloss for my kitchen and bathroom, it wipes down easier.

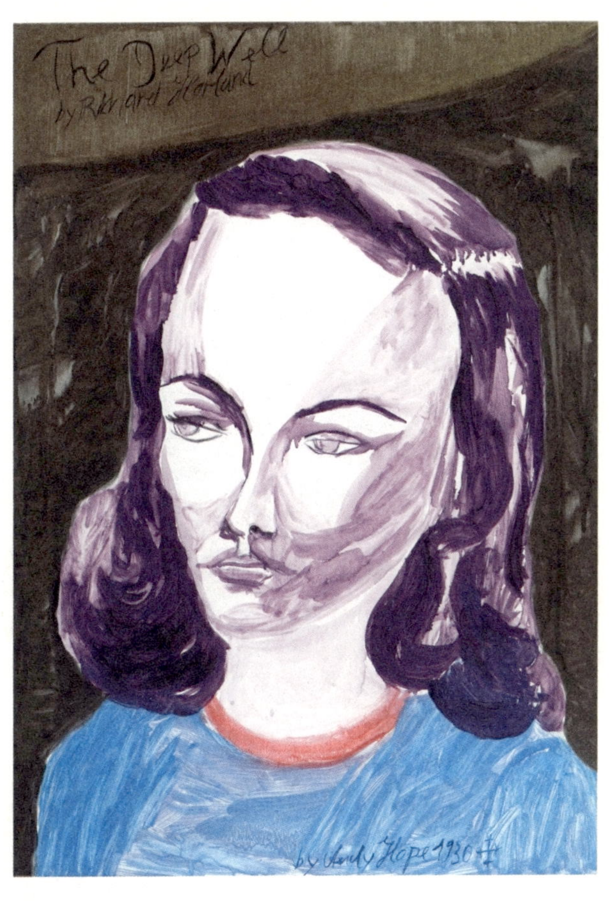

Andreas Hofer, *The Deep Well*, 2010

Andreas Hofer, *A for a Pleasant Room*, 2007 →

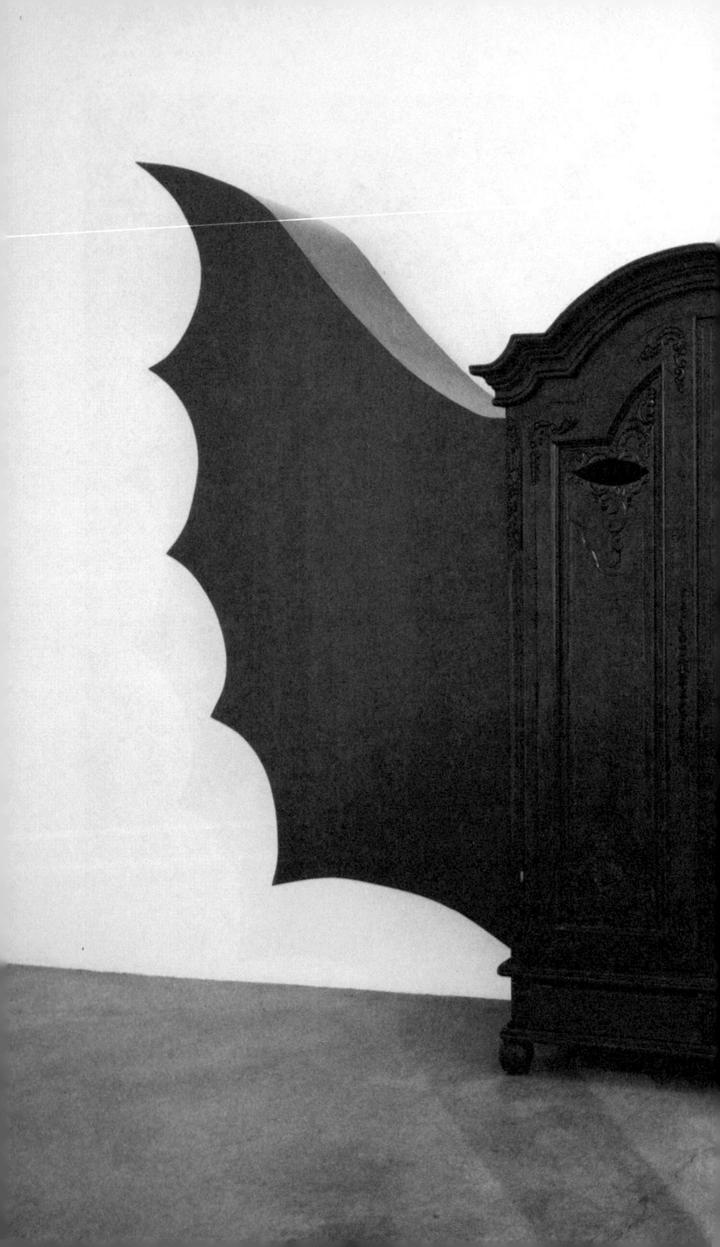

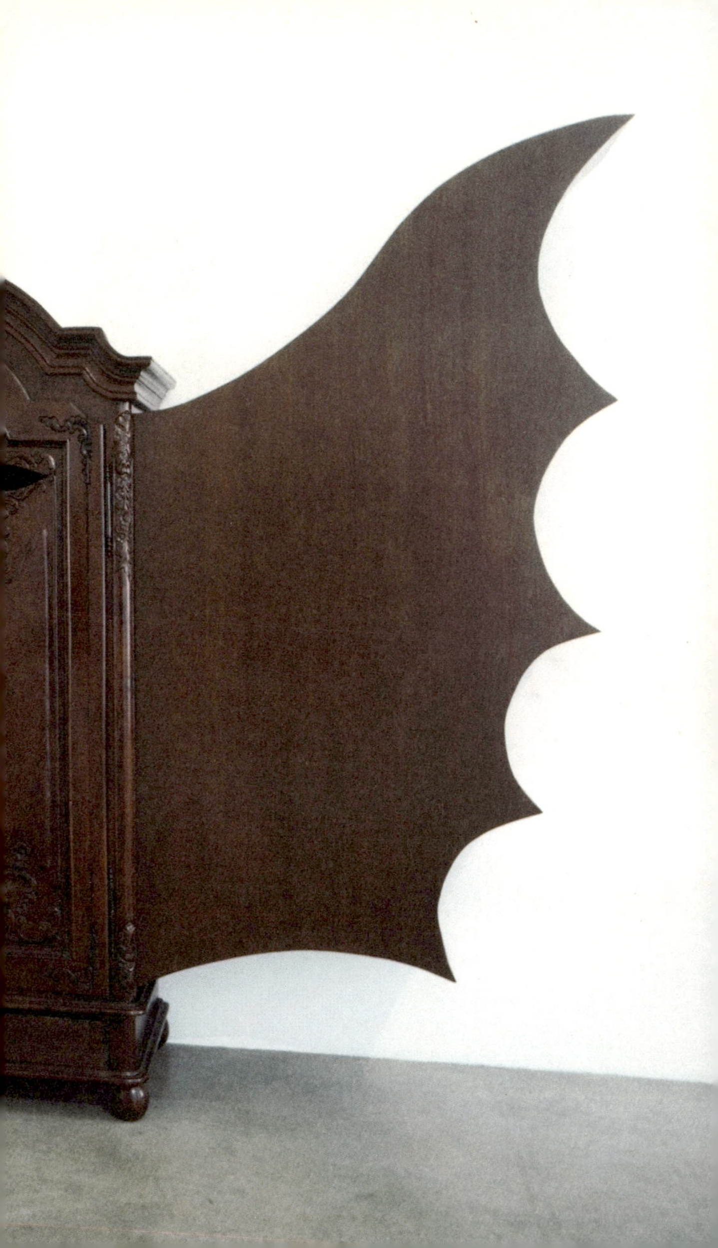

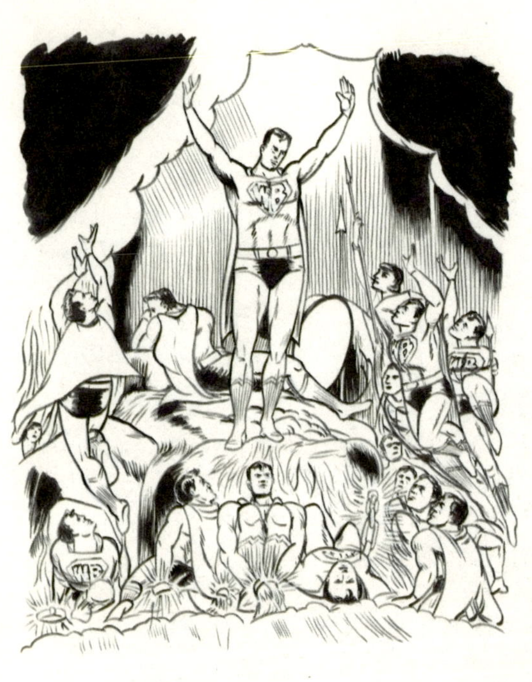

Jim Shaw, *Blake/Boring*, 2010

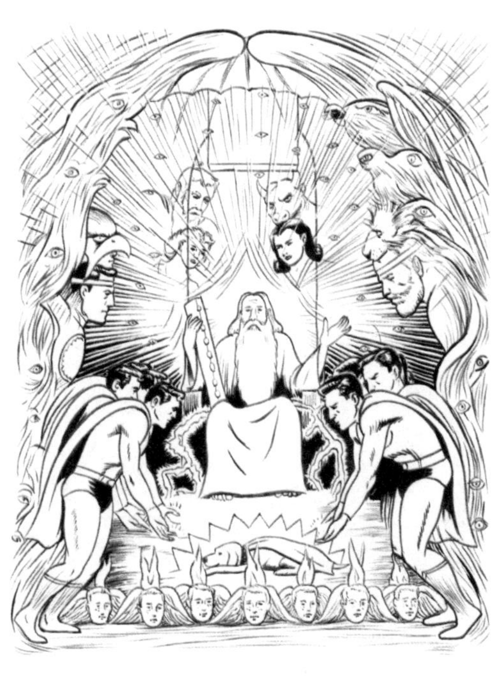

Jim Shaw, *Blake/Boring*, 2010

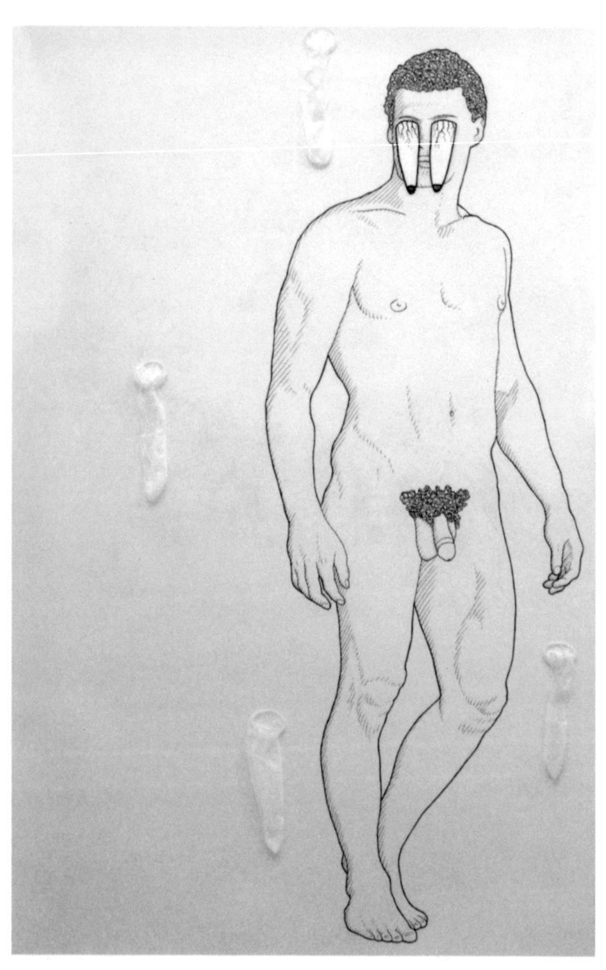

Jim Shaw, *Dream Object*, 2007

86

What role does psychoanalysis play for you, and in your production? What do you think of the qualification of a "missed rendez-vous" for defining the relationship between Surrealism and psychoanalysis?

JIM SHAW: I guess I try to psychoanalyze myself and our culture in my work. The new Superman work has some relation to the psychology and theology of corporate culture for instance. I think the Surrealists misinterpreted Freud similarly to 80s artists misinterpreting Baudrillard, but each came up with something interesting as a result.

ANDREAS HOFER: I think the "missed rendez-vous" was the best that could happen to both of the actors in that game. I just had a show at the Freud Museum in London, a very nice place, actually one of the most interesting museums in London, and you could call my take on the situation there a "forcefully missed rendez-vous" or a joyfully exaggerated clash of our two cultures: Freud's and mine. His collection of art is amazing and I used my own to invade his universe as the haunted counterpart of his ... It was about the possibility of letting the tensions, the uncanny, the feeling of disaster grow instead of calming it down.

ALEXANDRA BIRCKEN: I have a sofa in my studio ...

CHRISTIAN HOLSTAD: The brain is a terrible thing. Bodies never lie. Both Surrealism and psycho-analysis are brain-exclusive.

MEREDITH JAMES: It is very easy to apply a psychoanalytic reading to almost all of my work, because the imagery I use is so consistent with Freudian examples of symbolism. I think those images emerge out of my interest in a particular historical period that includes Surrealism.

DOROTA JURCZAK: Psychoanalysis plays no role for me. I am just enjoying my dreams especially the dark ones. Knowledge destroys mysteries, I prefer wondering.

JUSTIN LIEBERMAN: Psychoanalysis is a lens. It plays a huge role for me. But I don't have an analyst. That is because I am afraid to look too deeply within myself. I think it is possible that this rendez-vous HAD to be missed, and must continue to be missed. I say this because the true fusion of Surrealism and psychoanalysis would probably obliterate them both, or result in something dull. It is a certain distance that sustains the relationship. Artists must act from a place of subjective experience. Scientists must take a more objective, instrumentalized view. These roles are correct. The irresolvable nature of the clash is most interesting part.

RY ROCKLEN: When I was a kid my room was my sanctuary and my own little world. I fantasized about the things I would show the President (Reagan at the time) if he were to visit my room. As a kid I loved my bed, my blocks, and my dinosaur bones. My work today mines these vivid memories and feelings.

LUCY STEIN: Surrealism opened a can of worms but shut it again by being so narrative/illustrative. The Americans took the baton but got all mired in being anti-illustration and meta-narrative. There is still plenty of scope for fiddling around in the gaps since there could never be a Breton or a Greenberg hectoring you these days. Bacon probably made this rendez-vous best so far, but there are still exciting possibilities for Jakub Julian Ziowlowski and Amy Sillman being the most fresh and zeitgeistish examples I can think of from now.

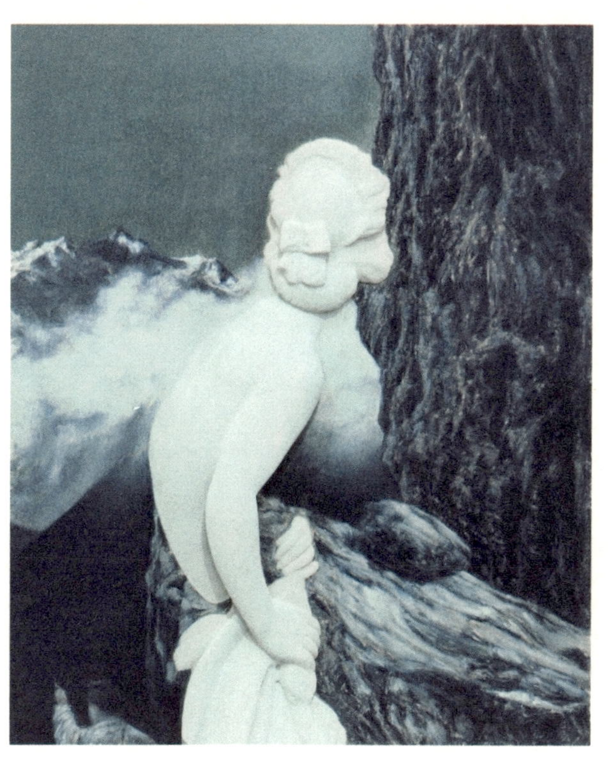

Cris Brodahl, *Aureole*, 2010

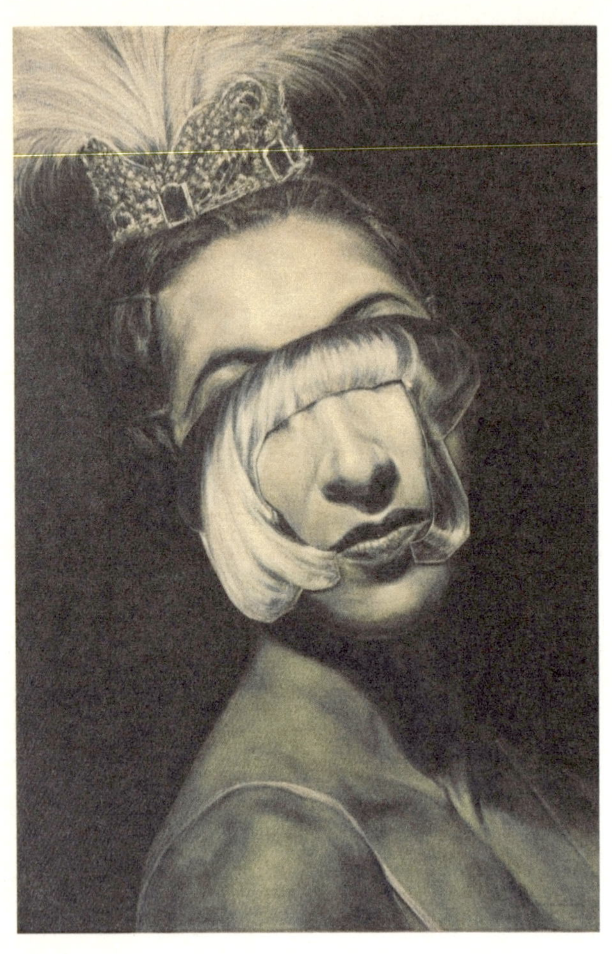

Cris Brodahl, *Dogmatics*, 2009

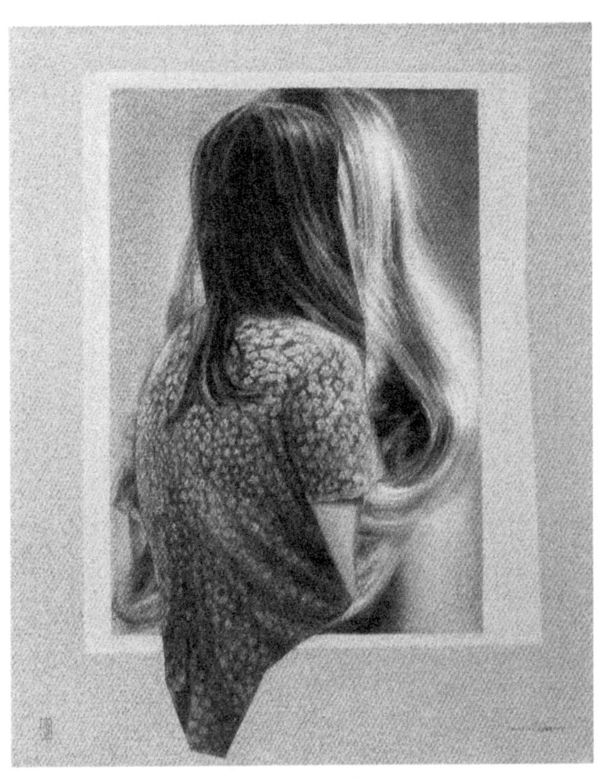

Cris Brodahl, *Tomorrow*, 2008

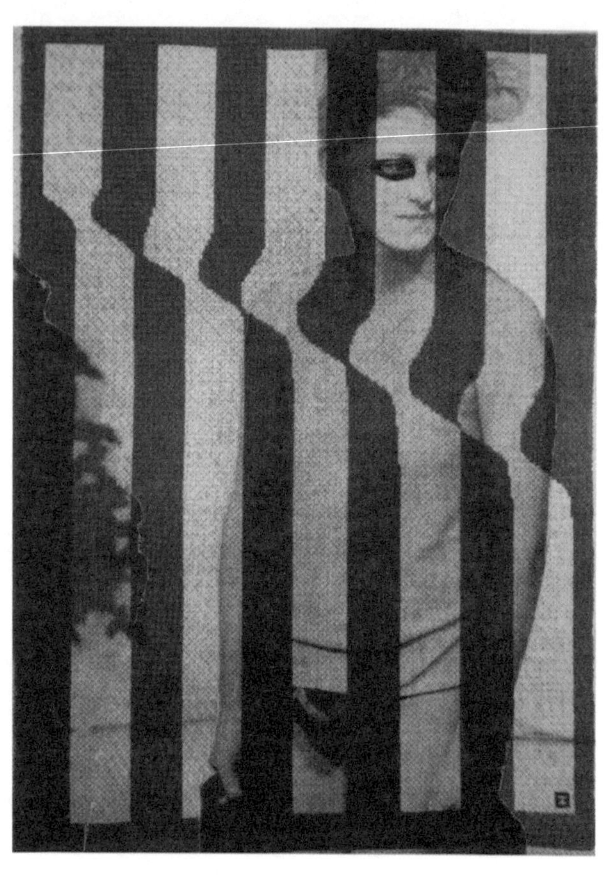

David Noonan, *Untitled*, 2009

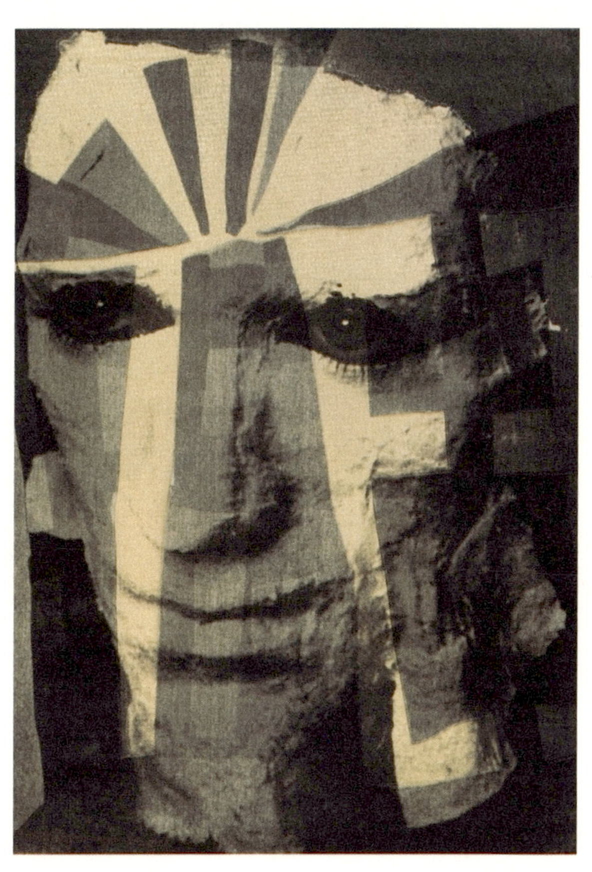

David Noonan, *Untitled*, 2009

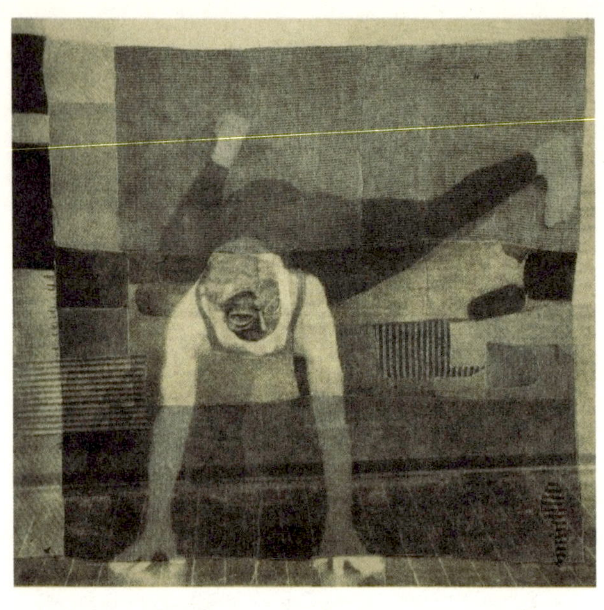

David Noonan, *Untitled (Orlando)*, 2010

You hated the 1980s (or not); what do you think of their resurgence today? Is this a necessary historicization or a simple repeat, a somehow degraded version?

STEVEN CLAYDON: The serpents of spectacle have got us all confused, have they not?

ALEXANDRA BIRCKEN: Resurging elements of passed times are never simple repeats as they are reinterpreted by those who did not live through the times first hand. It's like second-hand clothes ... 80s elements we see today are not even watered-down versions of the original because they are stripped of their political and social content and meaning. It's empty masquerade camouflaging a void.

CARTER: I love "Solid Gold" and Boy George was brave and an inspiration to me. As far as visual art, I always hated that Keith Haring had such a huge career. Robert Gober was also an inspiration, as was Jenny Holzer, the Starn Twins ... Charles Ray ... the list is long.

ROSS CHISHOLM: You should ask me after the election. I don't think I remember the 80s especially fondly. Growing up in it, I was probably too young to be engaged politically. As always, it was retrospect that contextualized the decade and made apparent its narratives. I don't think any resurgence today is a degraded version, nor a simple repetition, more a bastardized hybridization culminating in fashions I was too young to wear then and too old and self-conscious to wear now.

ANDREAS HOFER: I'm sorry, but don't you think the 1880s were even more hateful, and so was the official follow-up, the uniforms, that you call "necessary historicization, a simple repeat, a somehow degraded version?" We are approaching now 2014, the centenary of WW1, or the real catastrophe that happened to be the result of the love for uniforms in the 1880s!

DES HUGHES: I'm probably too old to notice the resurgence in music or fashion, but would imagine that it's as faithful to the original as "Happy Days" was to the 1950s. I think the art produced was the result of a particular unique set of circumstances and was as credible as that of any other era. I think its concerns with excess or ambition were as valid as ideas of economy or reduction explored at other times in history.

JUSTIN LIEBERMAN: I loved the 80s. That was my childhood. I experienced them mostly through TV though. I didn't know about the resurgence. Probably better for it to be a repeat than a historicization. I do not want to read the history of my childhood. I would rather experience a degraded version of it than see it set in stone. Shouldn't history take this form? Doing it again to try and get it right? Or to get it wrong again, but this time with feeling! Not standing back and rubbing our chins to decide what it was from our safe place at the end.

JIM SHAW: What is the 80s resurgence? I'd think the 70s anti-object-ism is more appropriate to today.

NICK LOWE: There is some art I really love from the 80s, like Ashley Bickerton and Albert Oehlen. It was the last decade before we relied on computers to make movies, send mail, record music, and absorb pornography, among other things. When did the computer age officially start? Maybe it hasn't even started yet. Maybe the computer age will officially start when we download files directly into the fiber of our brains.

TORSTEN SLAMA: Repetition is a way to secure continuous growth on a limited plane. To end this spiraling toward decadence, planetary colonization is needed. As an interim measure I would propose the taking of bold steps, for example, the offer of an incorporation of all nations of the African continent into the EU, thus creating a new super power; "Eufrica," which would hopefully mean not only new markets but new fashions.

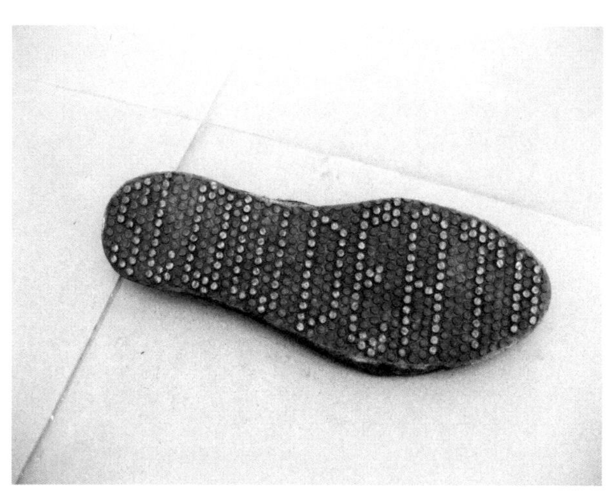

Richard Hughes, *Untitled*, 2009

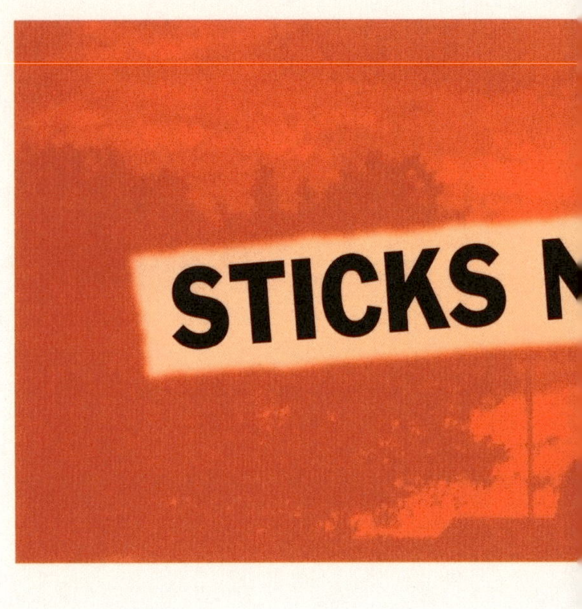

Larry Johnson, *Untitled (PIX PIX PIX PIX)*, 2010

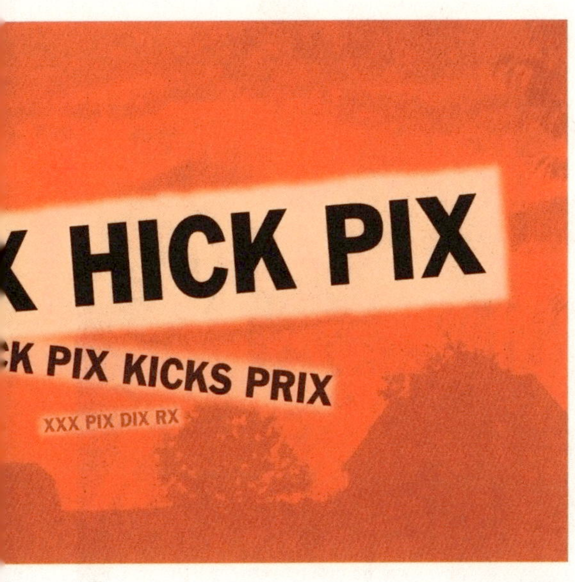
K HICK PIX
CK PIX KICKS PRIX
XXX PIX DIX RX

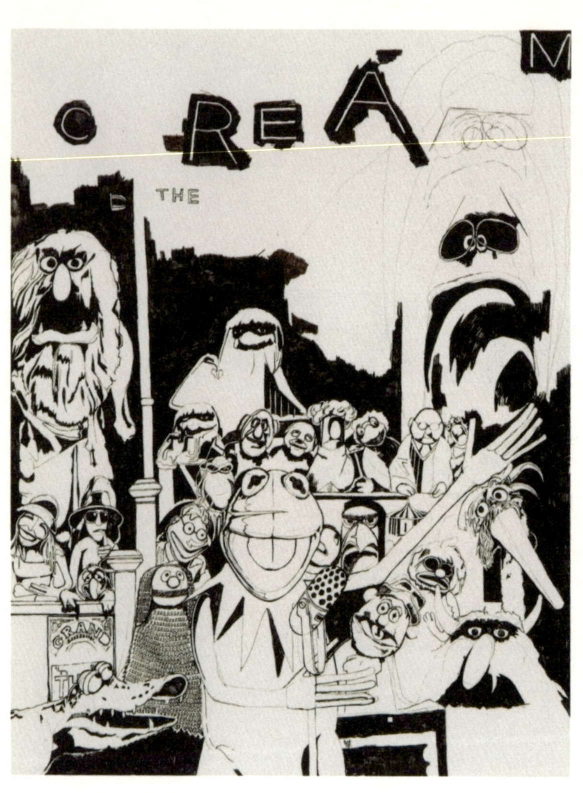

Nick Lowe, *The Muppet Show*, 2009–2010

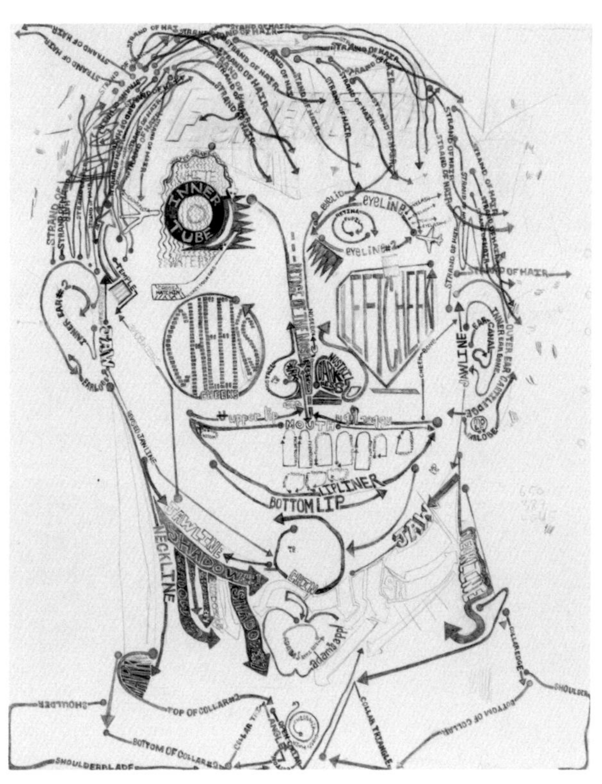

Nick Lowe, *Text Face*, 2007–2010

MARILYN DEAD

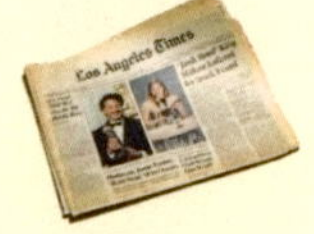

Larry Johnson, *Untitled (Cinema Moralia)*, 2010

In the 1990s, the group exhibition was sometimes conceived as a place to reformulate individual practices to affirm a more "collective" project. How do you relate to this idea? Do you envision the group exhibition as a possible "collaboration" with other(s) artist(s), as a (positive or negative) contamination of each other's work, as a competition, or just as any other exhibition's situation?

STEVEN CLAYDON: The majority of the shows you might be referring to were successful in the sense of a redefinition of practice because they where largely curated by artists or a collaboration between the artists and the curators. A group show's vices are artificiality in terms of alignment and their great strength is artificiality in terms of alignment.

ROSS CHISHOLM: The idea of cross-pollination is important in the production of my work. In my own practice, the different durations at play in the creation of different works can lead to an interesting rhythmic dynamic. The infusion of different works with different wavelengths can be incredibly fascinating. So it can be in group exhibitions. Obviously, you have less control over others work, but I think that adds an exciting jeopardy to an exhibition.

ANDREAS HOFER: I wouldn't say that this "(positive or negative) contamination" is a special 1990s thing or that it depends on that "group exhibition" condition: the interaction or collaboration or "collective project" or competition between individuals is always there. It's what artists do all the time, because we react to each other, to the living and the dead, to the animals and the stars.

DES HUGHES: Most artists probably recognize elements of collaboration, contamination, and competition when involved in a group show. Having made controlled decisions within discreet works, it is then necessary to move the threshold and consider this contamination as having an effect the work. I sometimes think that the rules of assemblage that apply to individual works could then be applied to installing within solo shows and even group shows.

MEREDITH JAMES: I conceive of my pieces as independent systems that play with particular sets of information, but I have been surprised at the affinities I find between my work and other works exhibited alongside it. It is moments like those when I feel like the work has exceeded my intentions for it.

DOROTA JURCZAK: I often work in collective projects, but this kind of group shows have an inner logic created by the artists who form that group before the show is set. There is no competition as there is no right or wrong in art.

JUSTIN LIEBERMAN: As artists, I think we are all "on the same side." I'm sure antagonisms between works will crop up. That will make the show interesting. I hope that my work can be contaminated. I have been told by many people that my work does not "play well with others" in group situations.

JIM SHAW: I hope my work won't infect anyone else's ... I'm slowly getting used to the idea of collaboration, but the time limit it takes just slips away.

JACQUES VIDAL: It all depends, I am a fan of shows curated by artists, where the art is looked at as a sort of raw material. I like this view of art trumping the laws of property and authorship, and that it represents a community in this way. Unfortunately, this is also one of the most difficult things to actually do, so I settle for appreciating a kind of compromise, where the curator becomes an artist and views the exhibit as the raw material ... Architectural customization as in Baldessari's Magrite show at LACMA, Gober's Menil Installation, Urs Fisher's recent group show in NYC (Shafrazi Gallery) ... I like the idea, to sum it up, that a curator will act as a physicist using the laws of the world to produce problems inherent to those laws. It is never a competition unless someone is slacking off; then they are decidedly the loser.

TORSTEN SLAMA: I like to think of an art show with several artists as a very limited art fair. I think curatorial efforts are currently very much in the danger of being overrated, while the possibility to focus on single works, regardless of the surrounding "positions," suffers.

NICK LOWE: John Baldessari always said that when you do a group show you should make a big heavy piece that is hard to move and set up early.

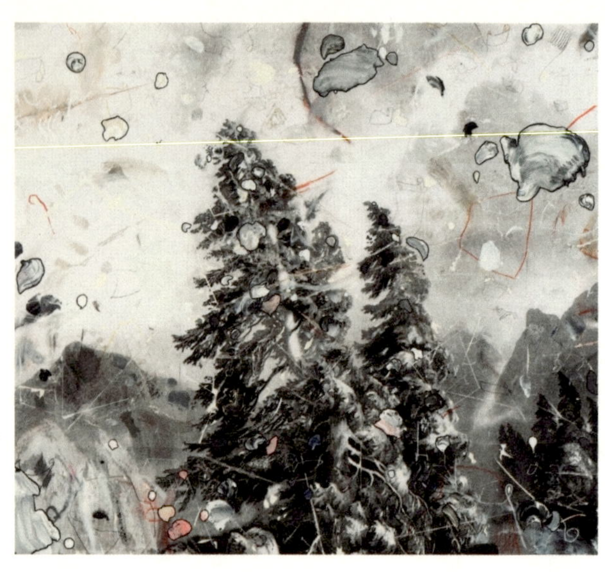

Carter, *Double Void (Although)*, 2010

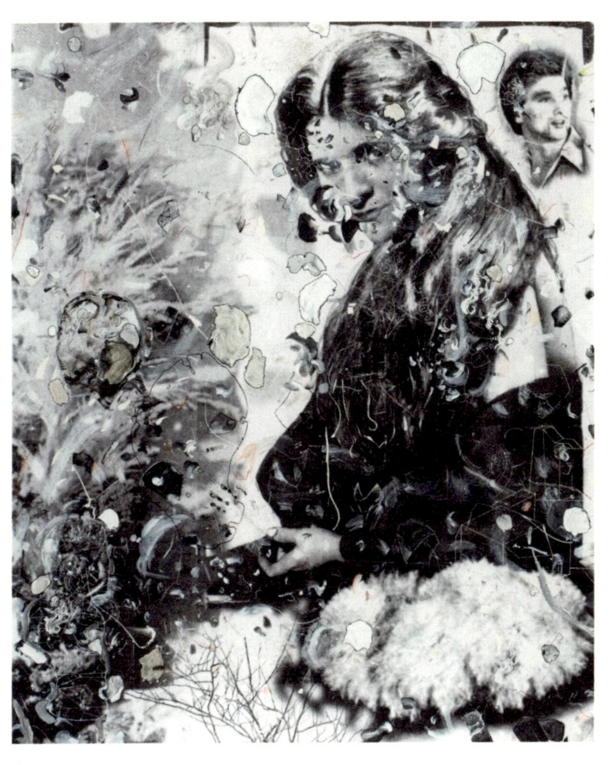

Carter, *The Past 100 Years*, 2009

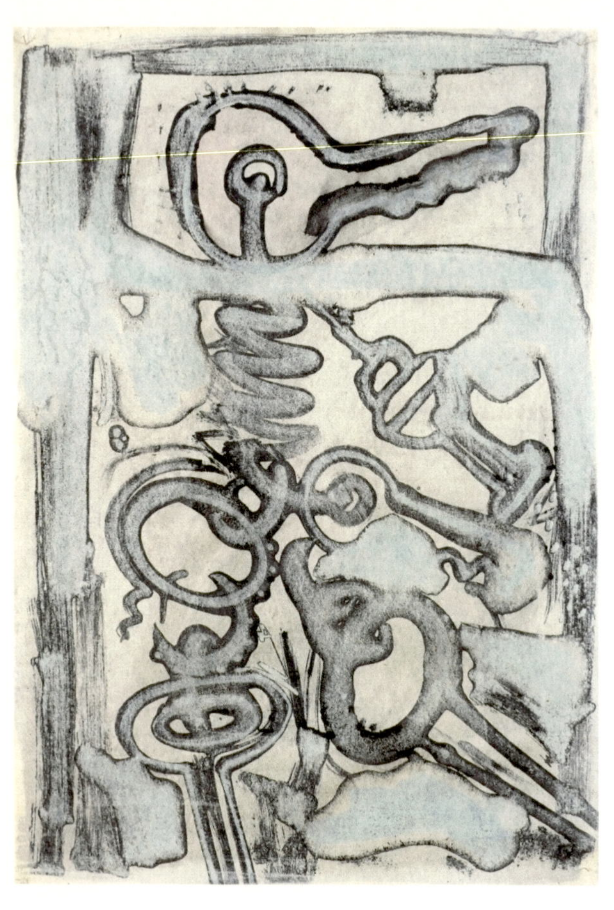

Stefan Thater, *Keys*, 2008

Stefan Thater, *Untitled*, 2005 →

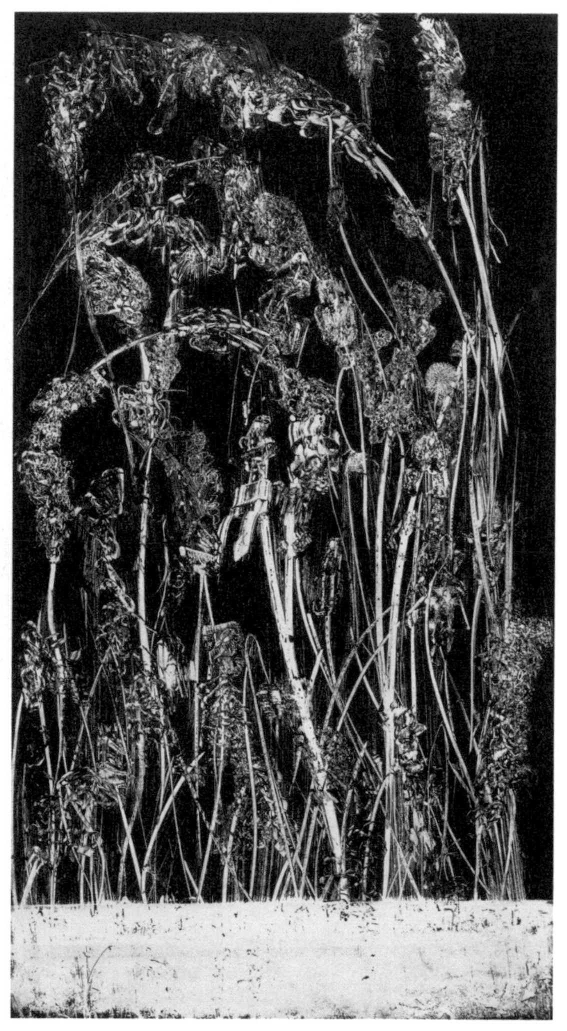

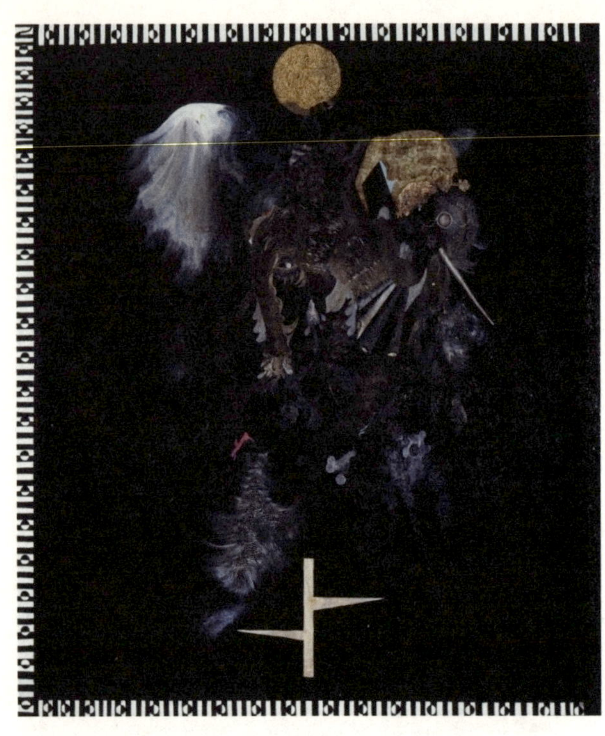

Michael Bauer, *MAARG VS. BOB*, 2010

Do you know the work of the other artists in the exhibition, and which one(s) do you particularly like or connect with?

STEVEN CLAYDON: The only things I have ever connected with have arms and legs.

ALEXANDRA BIRCKEN: Michael Bauer.

ROSS CHISHOLM: I saw Andreas Hofer's recent London exhibitions. I very much enjoyed his show at the Freud Museum.

SLAWOMIR ELSNER: I know some works of other participants and I do value them a lot. All of us are inspired by the same power but everybody deals different with it. This is how I like it.

CHARLIE HAMMOND: I have recently worked with Michael Bauer. I like him. We connected.

DES HUGHES: I'm familiar with several of the artists in the show and would like to think that I have stolen from all of them.

MEREDITH JAMES: My work is informed by conversations I've had with Justin Liberman and Jacques Vidal. I love picking their brains. Working in dialogue with other artists has proved a good way to generate ideas and find ways around the dead ends in any given train of thought.

CRIS BRODAHL: Love Sterling Ruby!

JUSTIN LIEBERMAN: I've watched the curation of this show take shape for a while. I like all the work of all the artists in it. The ones I know and the ones I don't. I am very happy to be included here.

JIM SHAW: I know a bit of the work of some of the other artists. Ry Rocklen was a student I worked with and I always did like his work. I tend to stay in my shell a lot and not go to shows. Between fatherhood and the time my work involves, I have very little time for gallery going.

JACQUES VIDAL: Steve Claydon is someone I want to discuss art with very much, I think he makes some unique decisions ... I know two of the artists very well: Meredith James always thinks on a scale that is unimaginable to me, her work is always a machine, and she is the boss. Also Justin Lieberman has always been an inspiration to me as an artistic steamroller, he smooths it out, I paint the lines on the road.

118

NICK LOWE: As artists, we are all very intensely connected, more so than any of us realize. There is this story I like about three astronauts that go up to the moon. When they get to the moon, one of the astronauts goes and looks for space rocks, one goes to photograph a crater, and one stays behind on the spaceship and does maintenance. All these astronauts are on the moon, each far apart, and they are so incredibly autonomous, each involved in their own individual activities. They all have the very unique experience of going to the moon but each person did a completely different thing on the moon. There are probably less people who have been to the moon than artists, but I like comparing art making to magic and space travel.

When you're invited to participate in a project, do you think that the location and the venue's characteristics play (or could play) an important role in the perception of your work? Do you take these characteristics into account while choosing the works to present at this venue? Do the clichés and the cultural experiences you have (or you are currently missing) of and in Paris interfere with your project's development for the current exhibition?

TORSTEN SLAMA: No.

ROSS CHISHOLM: The relationship between the work and the space can lead to exciting collisions. Location, duration, and intent are all factors in the works' epistemology.

A lot of the images I use have a type of cultural familiarity, such as the Gainsborough's and other society portraiture, and I think, for example, a move from London to New York adds a level of complexity to its reception, however incidental that is to its production. Having said that, I'm going to be working with Fragonard for Paris so we'll see.

CARTER: Of course venue/context/location is important. The way a work is shown is 50% of the puzzle. The placement. However, I've never created work for a particular location or audience. That's not something that interests me.

MICHAEL CLINE: I think I'm always hoping for some sort of cultural misunderstanding when showing outside of the US, but am always surprised to find more understanding abroad than at home.

ANDREAS HOFER: The location and the venue's characteristics are always very important to me—that's actually one reason to take part in this exhibition. And concerning the Paris-effect: there is certainly in Paris—maybe more than elsewhere—a strong sense of cliché, in the city itself and in the way the city today is dealing with art, which is more or less a compensation for the fact that Paris doesn't produce art anymore and lives in the past. So, what there is to do here is simply to give the city more of art that is unknown (which to a great part is the product of the ignorance of the people in power there).

MEREDITH JAMES: Most of my work is very site-specific: I either make the work in the space or change the space to fit the work. Here I am acting as though the venue is my suitcase, translating what might have been a large-scale video installation into something compact enough to carry with me on the plane.

JUSTIN LIEBERMAN: I suppose venue ALWAYS plays an enormous role in perception. However, this fact does not confer upon me a sense of obligation, because it is also the case that the work determines the perception of the venue. I will occasionally create works or exhibitions that are intertwined or conversant with their contexts in a specific way. Lately I have been trying to produce works that might become untethered from conventional ideas about context through a self-reflexive examination of my own past work. You might say that my own past work is the context in this case. This work seems to function in that way. It is more of an abstraction. I don't think this work is about Paris. Perhaps Paris will feel differently though. That would be fine with me.

JIM SHAW: I try to think what makes sense for any situation, group, etc. and hope not to merely trot out a Jim Shaw signature piece (if there is such a thing).

CRIS BRODAHL: There is this cliché of what is good, works everywhere. I am not so sure. It has to fit.

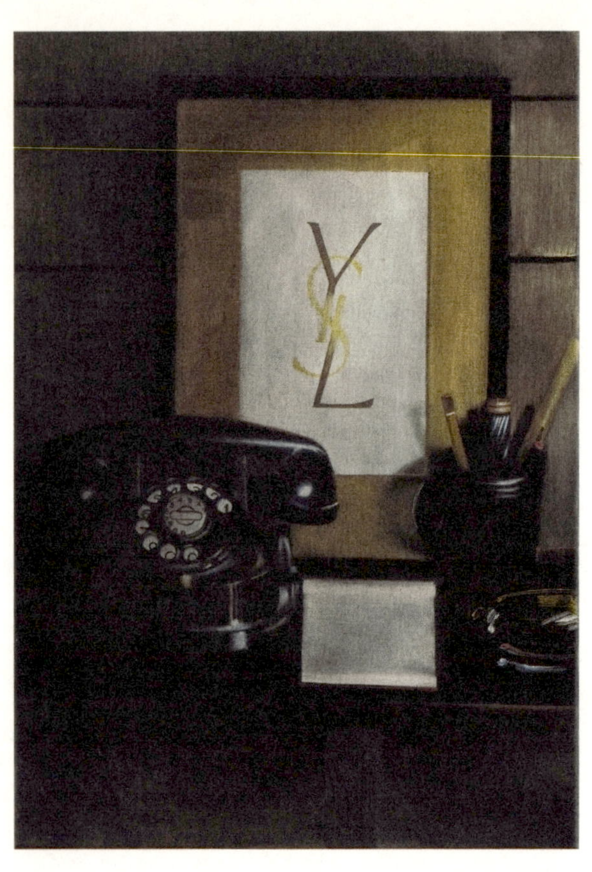

Slawomir Elsner, *Intérieur 01 (A.M.Cassandre)*, 2009

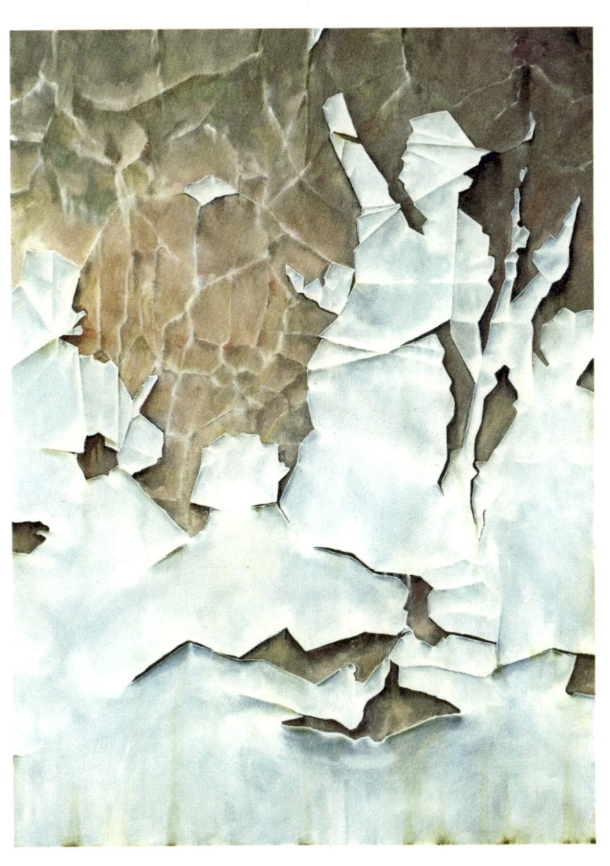

Slawomir Elsner, *Kalosze szczecia (The Galoshes of Fortune)*,
2009

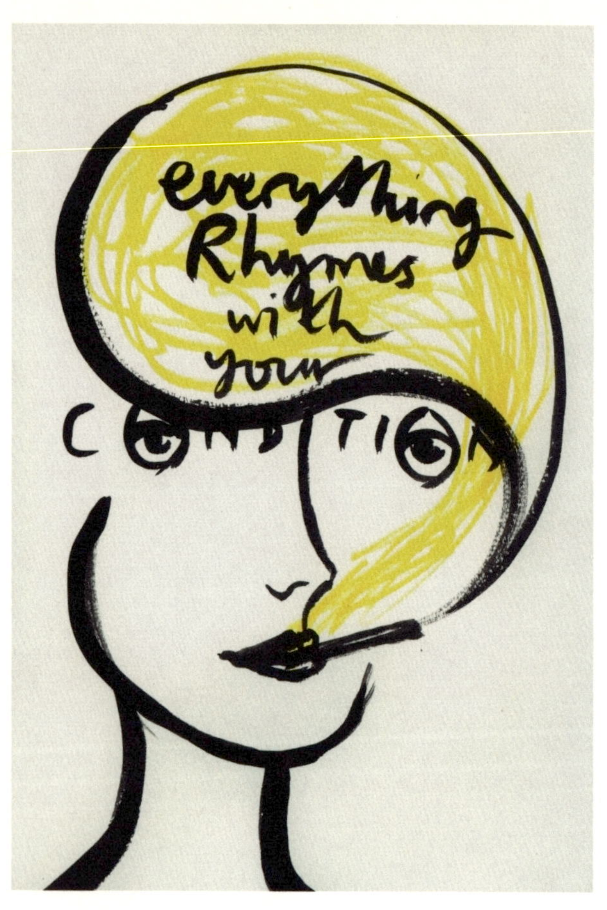

Lucy Stein, *Everything Rhymes with Your Condition*, 2010

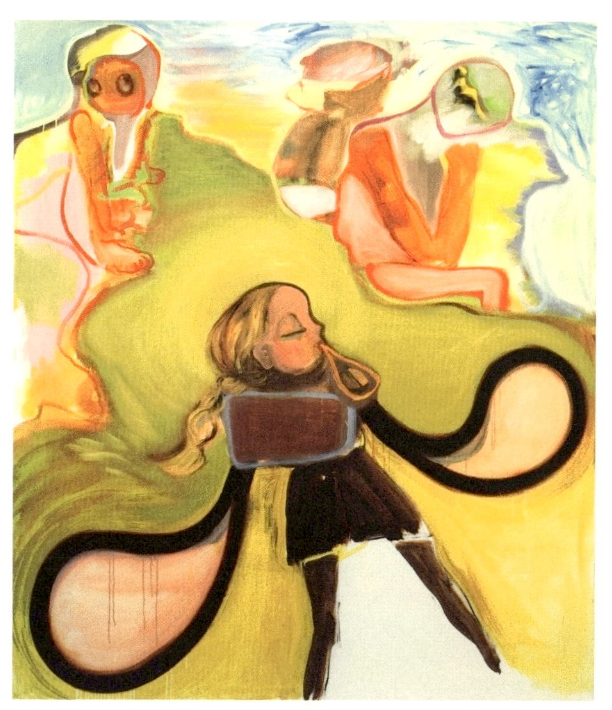

Lucy Stein, *Catherine Wheel*, 2009

Dorota Jurczak, *Lampa*, 2007 →

Dorota Jurczak, *Introligator*, 2010 →→

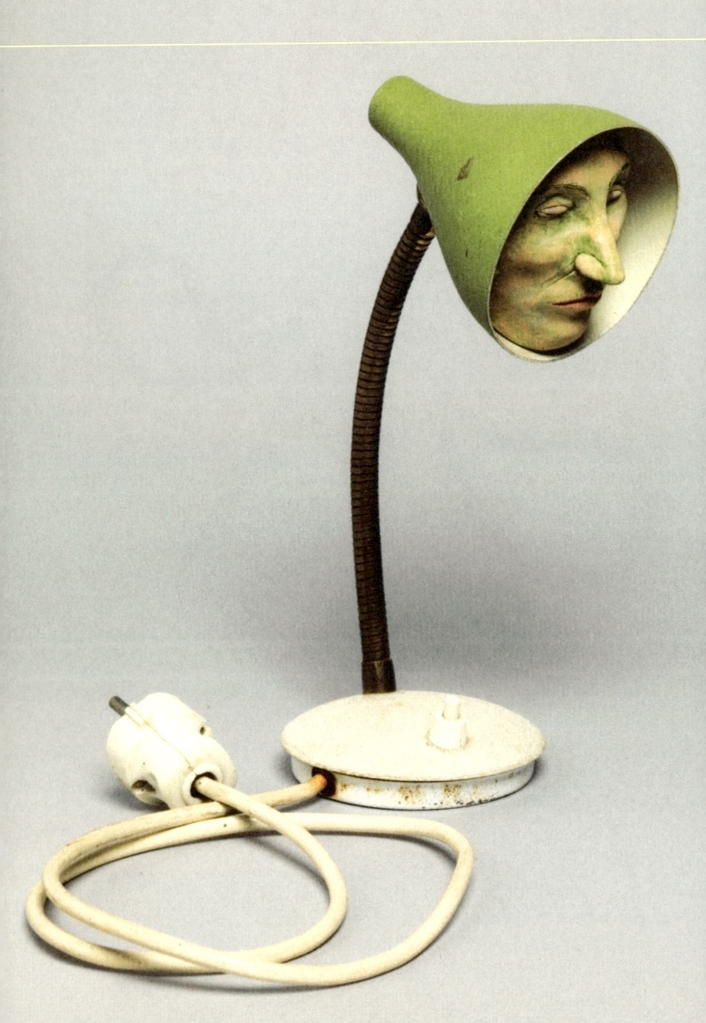

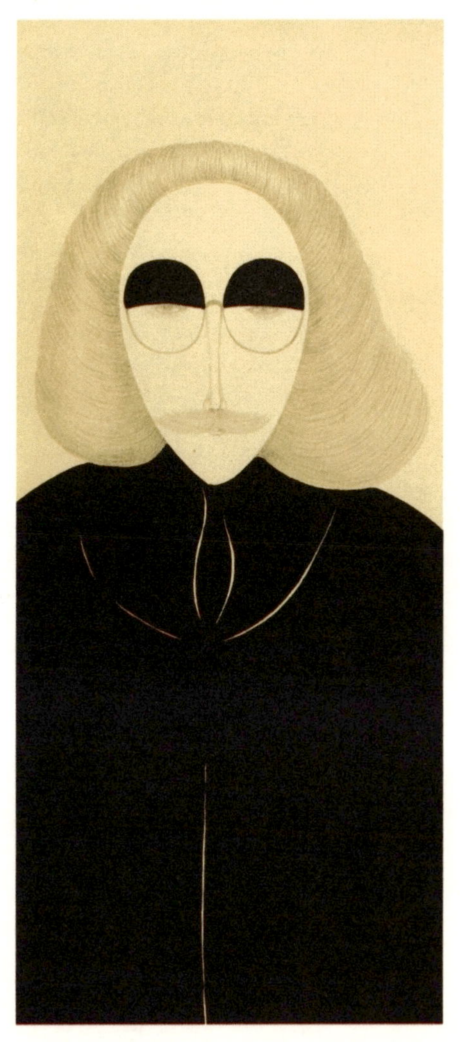

Justin Lieberman, *Either/Or*, 2010

Do you believe, as the critic Serge Guilbaut put it, that "New York stole the idea of modern art from Paris" after WWII? What do you think then of the development in the 1950s to 1970s of Situationism, electro-acoustic music, avant-garde cinema, or the nouveau roman and does this influence your relationship with Paris? How do you explain that the perception of the relationship of the city to contemporary art is so often negative?

STEVEN CLAYDON: I believe it has something to do with the closure of the catacombs.

MICHAEL CLINE: If it's negative, all the better. I tend to like crusty, overlooked, and undervalued things.

ANDREAS HOFER: (...) New York took over in the late 50s/early 60s simply because Paris wanted to get rid of the "idea" of modern art, or to be more precise: to get rid of the conditions that allow the production of ideas of modern art. The city destroyed all the favorable conditions that had made it the center of modern art for about 100 years. This destruction went very fast, efficiently, violently, and was full-blown. So New York took the gift without paying anything, maybe not even attention. And then, some two decades later, the city learned from Paris and went down the same path: destroying the favorable conditions for modern art, which had the same result. Now we see in New York the same problem: it's not producing any art anymore. The Situationists were the last "product" of the Paris-century and in a very bizarre way they—as they said themselves—kept the "Grail," but they also mystified the historical drama of that wonderful city, especially in their bad relation to art (an inability they shared with the city); they criticized art in the best way possible in their time, but they failed to continue art with their critique. So it's not only a perception that the relationship of the city to contemporary art is so often negative. It is a very, very real and regrettable fact.

CARTER: The only thing I know about Paris is the Louvre and that everyone speaks French and I don't, and that I can get a good cheese and mustard sandwich basically anywhere. So that's good. I love avant-garde cinema.

JIM SHAW: As an American student we saw very little European art of any country. Maybe the gridded, relatively spacious world of SoHo was closer to framing the aesthetic of postwar art than humanely proportioned Paris.

JACQUES VIDAL: From where I stand I understand that in recent times the difficulty of Paris for artists was similar to the one I had in New York, a simple question of money … Not enough time to make money and art, etc. It could be seen as a kind of artistic eugenics, this problem. I think New York inherited the "modern art" problem from Paris, a problem of people with intelligence and aspiration attempting to differentiate themselves from everyone else. I'll say that New York after WWII seems to have had the advantage of having little baggage about the prospect of making art, it was so unlikely as a profession that it was bound to seem more sincere, Paris may be in this advantageous position much more today—it could be an exciting time for the city again.

NICK LOWE: I had no idea what electro-acoustic music or the nouveau roman is, although I did find it out when I went on Wikipedia. Interesting. The more questions that people ask you, the more you learn.

TORSTEN SLAMA: "Stealing" in this context is nothing but an act of appropriation. If you are being robbed, there are reasons to question your security measures. Nouvelle vague cinema also would not have been possible without the critical reception of American film through French film critics, to my knowledge. The specific brand of electro-acoustic music in Paris had surely much to do with the realization that the French language had become a lost cause ... One thing unifies the whole of Europe, and even the French with the Germans: the realization that it was not the resistance of the powers of the European continent, but the unstoppable economy of the USA, unified with a sort of outrage and fierce motivation on the side of the British, that won the war in the West. This must have been a great shock especially to the French. This humbling experience explains many weaknesses and virtues of European avant-garde efforts after the War.

JUSTIN LIEBERMAN: First, I think it is important to point out that these things all had American analogues. They probably had Khazakhstani analogues, for all I know. It is easy to point to a marginalized American creative class, whose work was experimental, radical, etc. But why turn it into a competition between Paris and NY? The very nature of these ideas is an essentially inclusive one. That is to say, if you want to be in on one of these movements, if you feel moved by it and you want to participate, you need only follow its precepts and produce something of your own. Because if an aesthetic continues to be useful or productive in a broad sense, we can then assume it was not entirely staked on its place of origin or authorship. If we continue to insist on "first-ness," we simultaneously scrap the ideas themselves. Better to keep them.

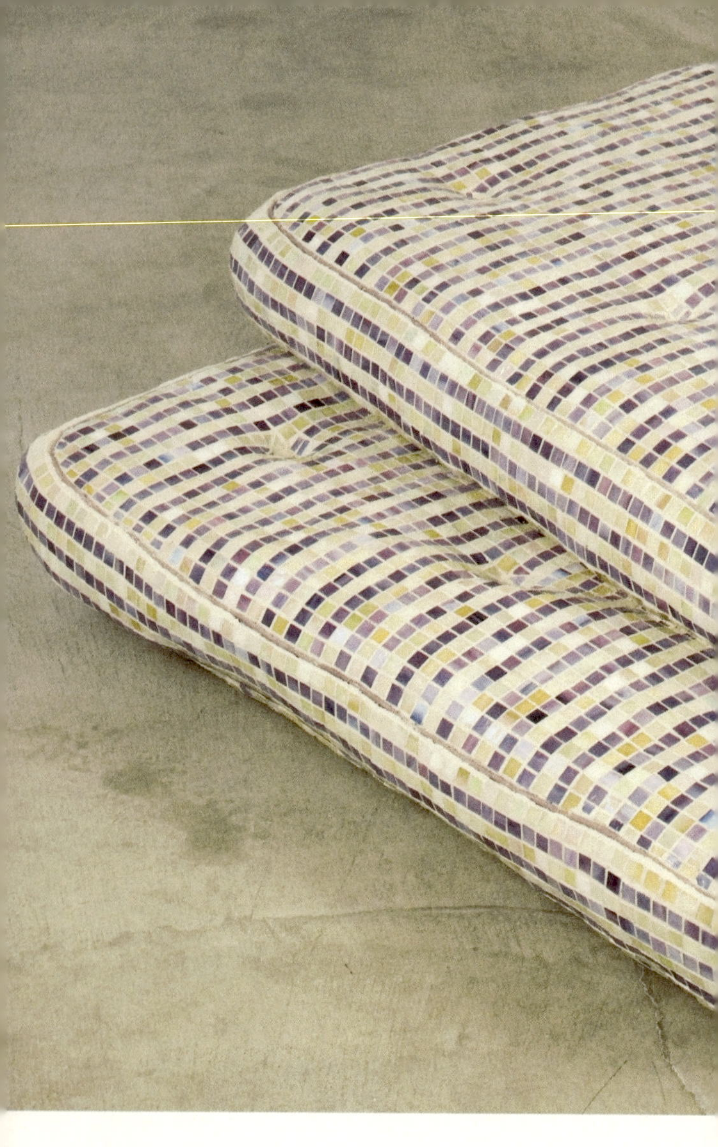

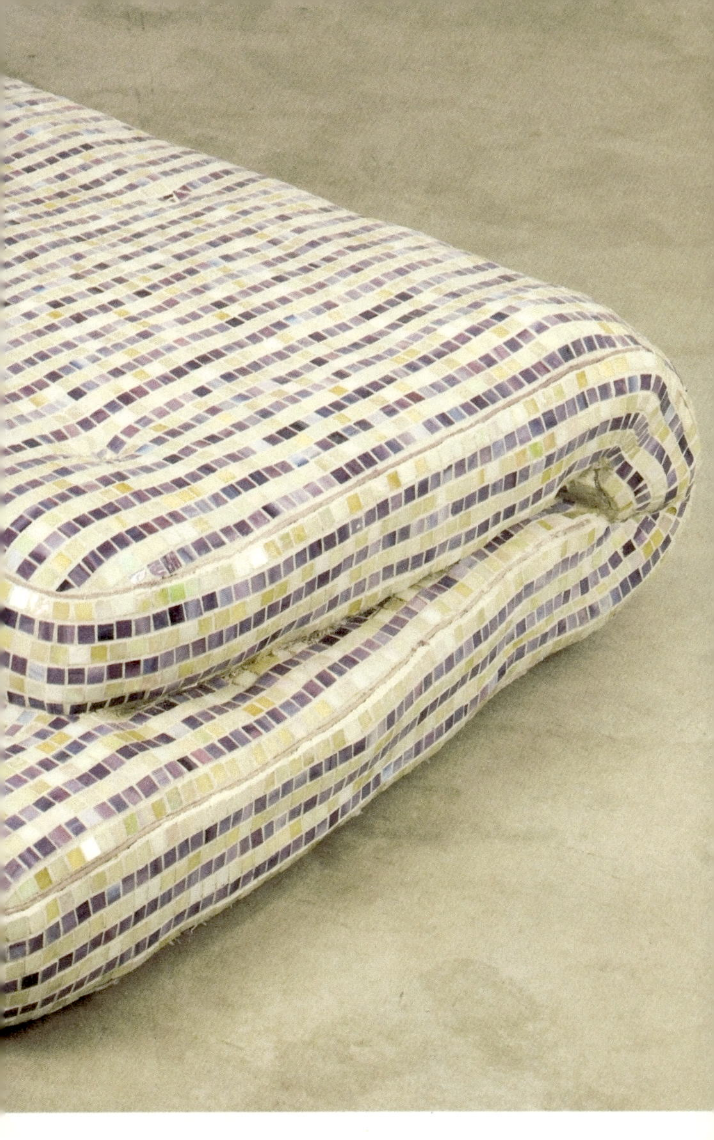

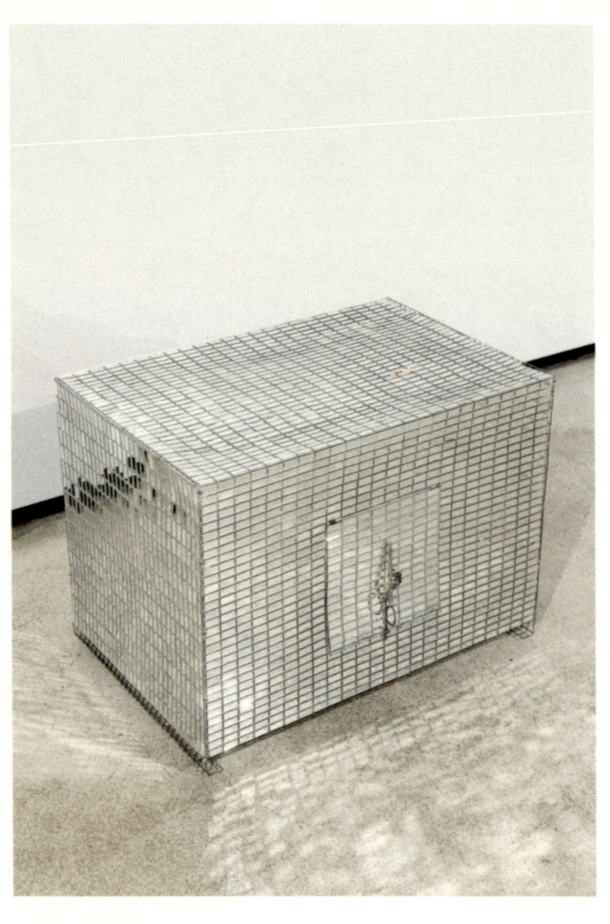

← Ry Rocklen, *On the Fourth Day*, 2009

Ry Rocklen, *My Delorean 2*, 2010

What project(s) are you developing for the exhibition?

SMITH: I am looking at this section of a gnarly telephone pole and trying to figure a way to give it limbs—then I'll remove them from the body of the pole. I'd like the body of the pole to be accessible at Alaïa and the limbs to end up somewhere separated. Want to keep this as blank and blunt as possible—just this gunked pole with missing parts. Maybe a stool as well for resting.

STEVEN CLAYDON: I am producing two new works that will inhabit two locations.

CARTER: I'm creating these really great glass sculptures. Life-sized busts. They are a continuation of paintings and sculptures that I've been working on for the past 20 years. I am very excited about them. Once they are finished they will sail or fly across the Atlantic, land in Paris, and be placed on display. The fact that this is even possible is mind-blowing to me. The Atlantic Ocean is vast. The sculptures will be created in America and will be shown in Europe. I like that.

MICHAEL CLINE: A painting.

SLAWOMIR ELSNER: I will contribute some pieces that reflect on Paris as a venue but all of my work is related to the world as a whole, after all.

CHRISTIAN HOLSTAD: Dreamcatchers.

MEREDITH JAMES: I am going to make a video of a scene from the book *The Invention of Morel* by Adolfo Bioy Casares. The scene takes place in an enclosed hexagonal room, in which the protagonist discovers machines that project the past onto the present. The final video will be composed of two layers of video: two separate sets of footage will be projected onto the same screen. The hexagonal room will also be present.

JUSTIN LIEBERMAN: I'm making some weird pieces in which I'm trying to shift my ideas about my own role in the work. My work has always been pretty reactive. Sometimes to the point of being pre-emptive in accounting for possible interpretations. Lately I've spent a lot of time with Mallarmé and Hart Crane. I like the way these poets' work reacts to *itself*. It is almost as if there is no reader at all. This opens up a space for ambiguity and experimentation while still allowing for the development of intricate structures that seem to produce meaning on their own. But in order to access this fusion, I have really had to take my own place in the work for granted to a certain extent. The result has been some things that are quite a bit more like art than my work in the past. I would not assume a false modesty about these pieces. They are quite good.

JIM SHAW: Black and white ink drawings and paintings that investigate the theme "Not Since Superman Died."

JACQUES VIDAL: I was struck immediately by the light in the spaces, and I'm attempting a series of sculptures, collages, and drawings which hopefully will produce a kind of vacuum for this. Flat black drawings, sculptures underneath the stairs that emit light, and collages of figures from the past.

NICK LOWE: I have been struggling to introduce text into my work. A friend of mine said, "the thing you're avoiding in your art is the thing that would be most interesting if it actually got worked out." I came up with a solution for incorporating text into image in my last solo show and I am expanding for the show in France. I am just going to "riff" on that. Riffing seems like it is a distinctly American phenomenon, I get the sense that France isn't a particularly riff-based culture.

STEFAN THATER: One thing that I would like to show in Paris is a new series of drawings. The painter Amelie von Wulffen, a friend of mine, just published a catalogue with self-portraits. I overworked these self-portraits by painting and drawing telephones over them. So the atmosphere of concentrated self-observation and silence (in the studio) is disturbed from the outside by paintings of ringing telephones. These machines take over the whole image and their cables are leading out of the picture frame. As well as that I would like to show paintings with lines, cables, and lots of stuff on them, technical and organic things, text substitutes.

CRIS BRODAHL: Bas-relief.

LUCY STEIN: POLVENTON (The Lost Art of Convalescence). I wrote a comedy-ish script set in a convalescent home for a film that Shana Moulton and I want to make at "Polventon," the beautiful modernist house that my grandfather built in North Cornwall. Since the owners recently told me to fuck off we have had to change our idea for the film and I have decided to somehow lean on the script and imagery for this exhibition, as there is scope for a lot of my paintings, drawings, and collages within the wider idea of "The lost art of convalescence." This is a subject close to my heart, especially since I feel more and more out of kilter with modern life where as an artist, speed of production, personal availability, and ability to perform hold more currency than concentration and thoroughness. I need a lot of time to think. I can't make my work in the back of a taxi and I won't be answering my phone if I'm working and that means at night too, 'cos at night I'm thinking. Anyway, in the script the characters are Gethsemane (she came to me in a dream while I was in Syria!), wasp girl (a very young and very startling prostitute I encountered in Spain who looked a lot like Kirchner's "Marzella"), the Omega Three (a chorus who speak only in aphorisms and malapropisms), the male hysterics, Gudrun Brangwen from *Women in Love*, and a male nurse. There will be boiled eggs and plane hugging. The works in the vitrines will be scattered with dead wasps, since the annual late August wasp invasion of Berlin will just be over. This will be a symbolic homage to Simonetta Vespucci, an old muse and acquaintance of mine who is usually depicted with the wasps of the Vespucci family flying around her head, and of course wasp girl/Marzella. The palette will be gulfstream bright and pastel or waspish black and yellow. Everything will be chic. We'll see ...

Michael Smith, *Untitled*, 2009

Meredith James, *Day Shift*, 2009 →→

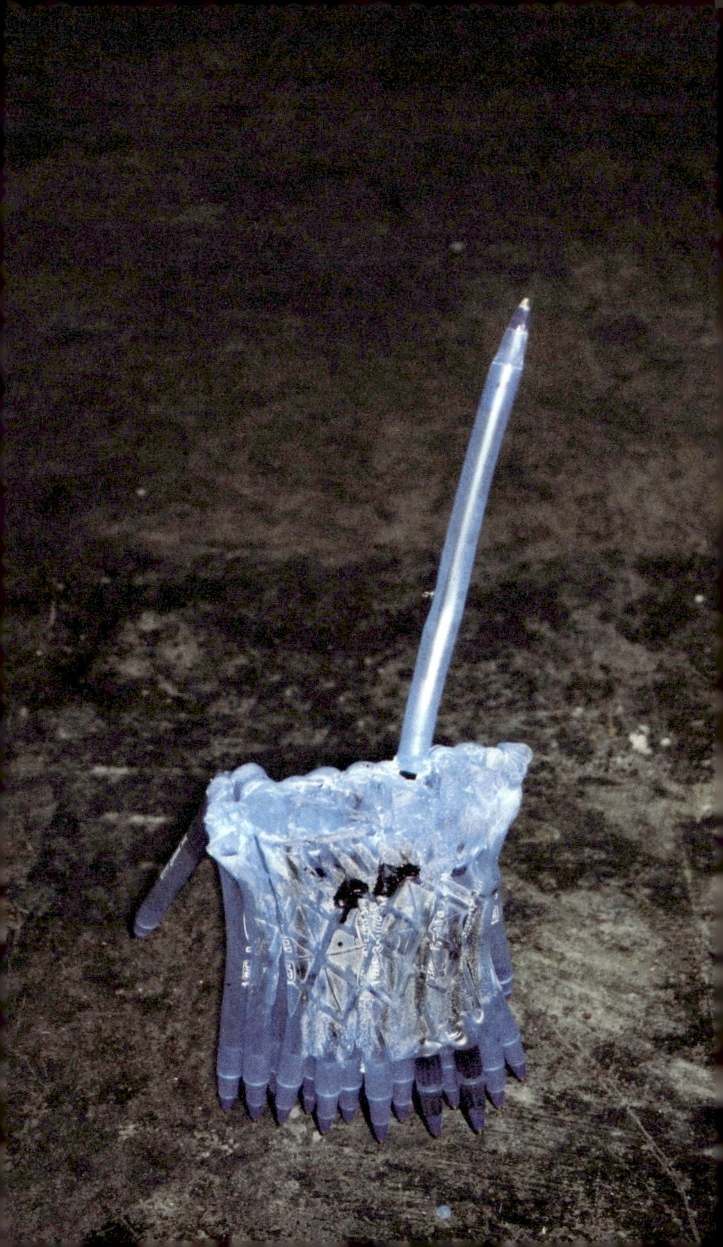

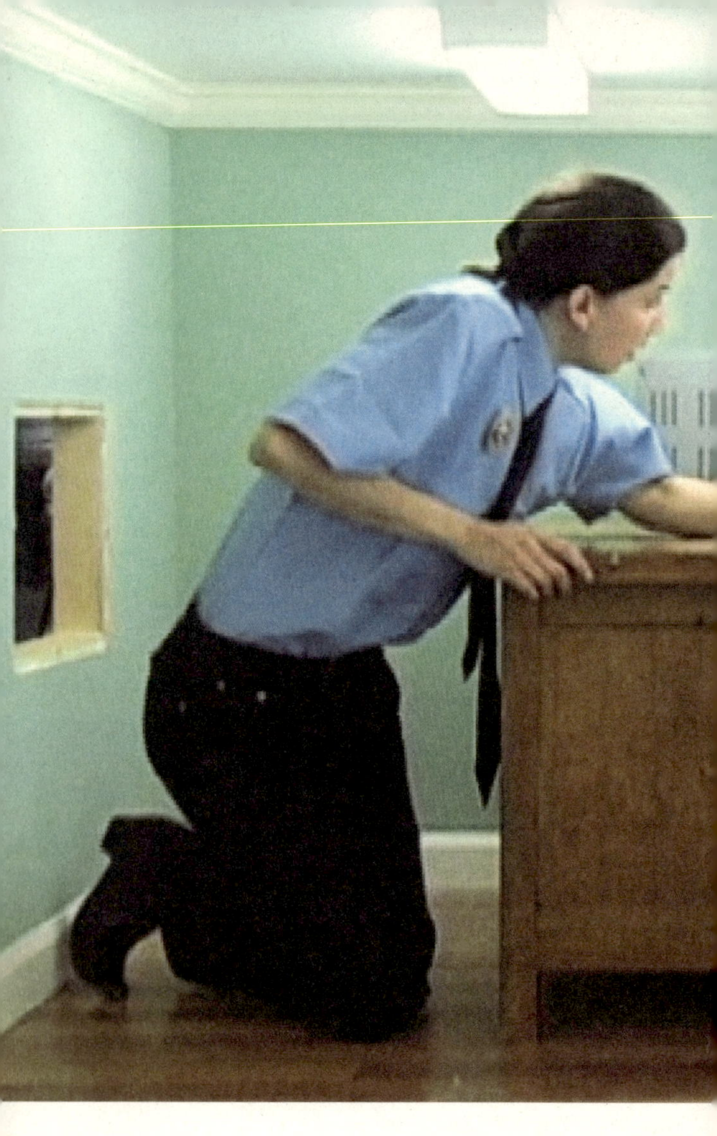

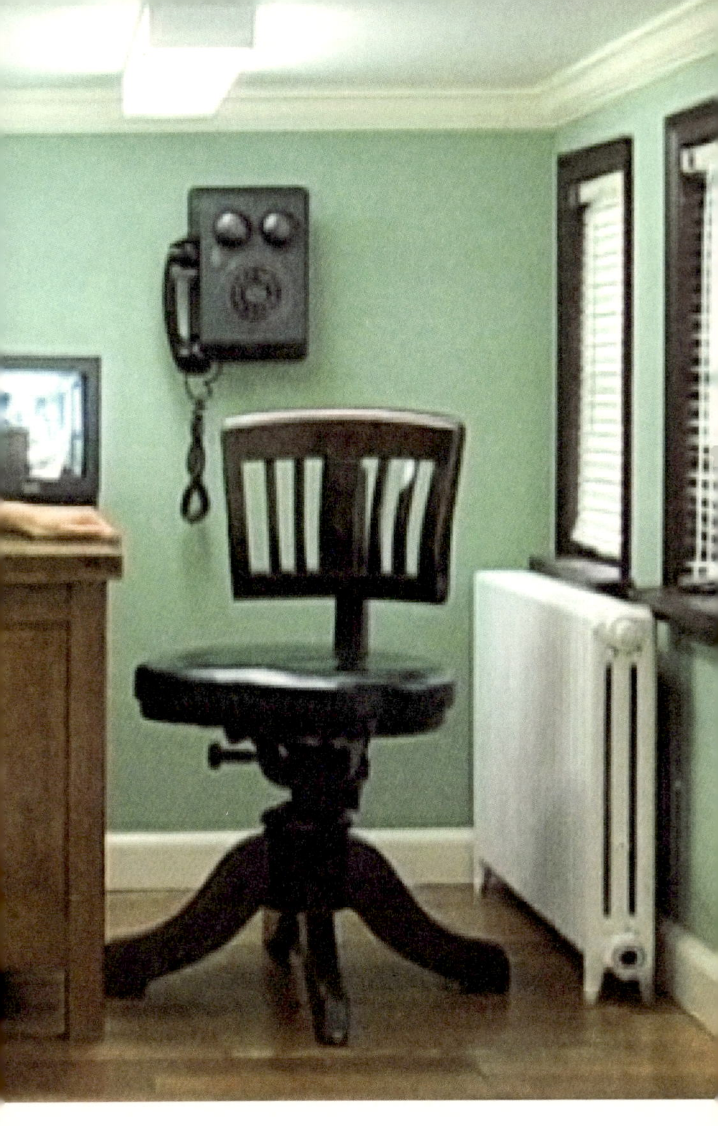

Afterword

Marc Jancou

It is only July, and yet my mind has leapt forward to September, to Paris, where I will present 27 artists at six exhibition sites on both banks of the Seine. In my mind, I play with the six sites like a game of Monopoly; I fit them together like Lego bricks, 1, 2, 3, 4, 5, 6. Counted altogether, I have the largest exhibition space in the city to play with.

Time is passing; I have an hourglass constantly in my mind's eye. I have been working on this exhibition for a year or more. It seems like ages. I'm feeling my way forward, slowly, through trial and error. Parisians and their mannerisms, their words, are fascinating—I watch everything, I listen to everything; I understand sometimes.

I was in Geneva in 2008 with my friend Marc Blondeau, who offered me the marvelous gift of hosting an exhibition for me. I thoroughly enjoyed putting the exhibition together, and it was a success. It has left memories and a title that I still find amusing—*In Geneva No One Can Hear You Scream*—and an eponymous beautiful book.

I feel as if every book I publish is a gift to myself. Geneva feels so far away now. It was more straightforward: I invited 15 artists and everything was together on the same site. For Paris, I have brought together 27 artists on six sites, two on the Right Bank and four on the Left, each arising from an encounter with an exceptional individual: Azzedine Alaïa, Jean-Michel Camard, Louis Lefebvre, Catherine Houard, Louis Albert de Broglie, Etienne Breton, and again Marc Blondeau. It's intended to be a stroll or course through Paris, as I usually explain to people. For me, it's become more of an obstacle course.

Will it awaken people's curiosity? Will they knock on the door at the six addresses and see everything there is to see? I catch myself daydreaming. Go for a stroll: take your time, find one of the exhibits, then go back out into the street in the heart of Paris, look up at your surroundings, and head off to the next address, or cut class by stopping off at a sidewalk café. And then move on again, moving forward. Lose yourself in the crowd for a few moments. This downtime—the time between exhibition sites—is also part of my exhibition: remembering what you have just seen and looking forward to what else there is to see. Time and movement. Bridging art and everyday life.

I am betting on beautiful weather. Will the weather be fine? It has to be. Is the weather fine in Paris in September? Always? For the past hundred years? I'll have to look up the weather statistics ... It would be great if people could stroll from one site to the next like free electrons, with the catalogue in their hand or pocket, like a tool for thought, a simple, compact, rich source filled with signs and things to read and see. With the help of my friend Lionel Bovier, I prompted the artists to speak by asking them 12 questions. I'm impatient to see the finished book. What will it look like? I have no idea, but I love the wait. I love producing books almost as much as curating exhibitions. If I weren't running a gallery, I'd own a bookshop. I swear, in my next life I'll be a bookseller and live surrounded by thousands of books.

I thought about traveling around Europe; that would keep me busy and prevent me from staying in my gallery in Chelsea, New York, like a shopkeeper behind his counter. That's it, I'll travel all over Europe, from north to south, organizing exhibitions here and there. Keep moving, seeking out new artists, meeting new people. Dreaming and making other people dream. I'll catch myself musing that art changes the world in a more beautiful way.

Biographies and captions

Born in 1973 in Erkelenz (Germany), **Michael Bauer** lives and works in Cologne.

[p. 116] *MAARG VS. BOB*, 2010
Oil on canvas; 23.5 x 19.75 inches
Courtesy Lisa Cooley, New York

Born in 1967 in Cologne (Germany), **Alexandra Bircken** lives and works in Cologne.

[p. 20–21] *Icarus Survivor*, 2009
Plaster pigments, silver, brass, steel, wood, metal, spray paint, wool, synthetic fibers, cotton, plastic, glue, and thread;
55 x 54 x 9.5 inches
Courtesy of Herald Street, London, and BQ, Berlin

[p. 22] *Containerland*, 2009
Plaster, cardboard, fabric, toilet roll, Lego, earring, photograph, eraser, yarn, clothing, plastic containers, wax, and acrylic;
17.7 x 15.7 x 15.7 inches
Courtesy of Herald Street, London, and BQ, Berlin

Born in 1963 in Ghent (Belgium), **Cris Brodahl** lives and works in Ghent.

[p. 91] *Aureole*, 2010
Chemical porcelain and oil paint;
12.6 x 9.84 inches
Courtesy of Xavier Hufkens Gallery

[p. 92] *Dogmatics*, 2009
Oil on glued linen; 29.5 x 19.7 inches
Courtesy of Xavier Hufkens Gallery

[p. 93] *Tomorrow*, 2008
Oil on glued linen; 24 x 19.7 inches
Courtesy of Xavier Hufkens Gallery

Carter lives and works in New York.
www.carteroffice.com

[p. 112] *Double Void* (Although), 2010
Digitally altered and dated landscape on folded and defaced laser prints, acrylic ink, acrylic paint, pencil, colored pencil, and gel medium on paper and on canvas;
30 x 34 x 3 inches
Courtesy of the artist, Marc Jancou Contemporary, New York, and Salon 94, New York

[p. 113] *The Past 100 Years*, 2009
Digitally altered, folded and defaced laser prints, acrylic ink, paint, and gel medium on paper on canvas; 86 x 72 inches
Courtesy of the artist and Salon 94, New York

Born in 1977 in London (England), **Ross Chisholm** lives and works in London.

[p. 40–41] *Urn*, 2010
Oil on canvas, 4 panels, each:
11.81 x 7.87 inches
Courtesy of the artist, Marc Jancou Contemporary,

New York, and IBID Projects,
London

Born in 1969 in London (England),
Steve Claydon lives and works
in London.

[p. 38] *League Diptych*, 2009
Powder-coated steel, Buckram,
acrylic and oil on canvas, wood;
dimensions variable
Courtesy of the artist and HOTEL,
London

[p. 39] *Won from Coarseness*, 2009
Glazed ceramic, concrete, painted
and lacquered bamboo, mild steel,
ferric, brass, wood, hair, powder-
coated steel, artist's T-shirt;
27.56 x 92.52 x 55.91 inches
Courtesy of the artist and HOTEL,
London

Born in 1973 in Florida (USA),
Michael Cline lives and works
in New York.

[p. 55] *Fenced*, 2009
Oil on linen; 66 x 46 inches
Courtesy of the artist and Marc
Jancou Contemporary, New York

[p. 56] *New Age Signboard*, 2009
Oil on linen; 30 x 24 inches
Courtesy of the artist and Marc
Jancou Contemporary, New York

[p. 57] *A.H.*, 2010
Oil on linen; 40 x 30 inches
Courtesy of the artist and Marc
Jancou Contemporary, New York

Born in 1976 in Wodzislaw (Poland),
Slawomir Elsner lives and works
in Berlin.

[p. 124] *Intérieur 01
(A.M.Cassandre)*, 2009
Oil on canvas; 27.56 x 19.69 inches
Courtesy of the artist and Marc
Jancou Contemporary, New York

[p. 125] *Kalosze szczecia
(The Galoshes of Fortune)*, 2009
Oil on canvas; 90.55 x 66.93 inches
Courtesy of the artist and
Marc Jancou Contemporary,
New York

Born in 1979 in Aylesbury
(England), **Charlie Hammond** lives
and works in Glasgow.

[p. 69] *Portrait as a Bunch of
Rusty Keys*, 2008
Oil on canvas; 24.8 x 20.87 inches
Courtesy of the artist and Sorcha
Dallas, Glasgow

Born in 1963 in Munich (Germany),
Andreas Hofer lives and works
in Berlin.

[p. 81] *The Deep Well*, 2010
Oil on board, 27 x 19.38 inches
Courtesy the artist and Hauser
& Wirth

[p. 82–83] *A for a Pleasant Room*,
2007
Wood armoire, 147 x 87 x 21.5
inches
Courtesy the artist and Hauser
& Wirth

Born in 1972 in Anaheim
(California, USA), **Christian Holstad**
lives and works in Brooklyn.
www.christianholstad.com

[p. 42] *Portrait #3 (Upside Down
Can with Prosciutto and Melon,
a Bra, and an Empty Toilet Paper
Roll)*, 2009
Collage on paper; 40 x 60 inches
Courtesy of Daniel Reich Gallery,
New York

[p. 43] *Three Sacrifices*, 2007
Collage on paper; 40 x 60 inches
Courtesy of Daniel Reich Gallery,
New York

Born in 1970 in Birmingham (England), **Des Hughes** lives and works in Herefordshire.

[p. 37] *Dark Aged*, 2008
Cast resin with oxidized iron dust and fiberglass; 13.8 x 9.8 x 11.8 inches
Courtesy of the artist and Ancient & Modern, London

[p. 44] *Friend of the Friendless*, 2009
Cast resin, marble powder; 1.9 x 17.7 x 7.4 inches
Courtesy of the artist and Ancient & Modern, London

Born in 1974 in Birmingham (England), **Richard Hughes** lives and works in London.

[p. 101] *Untitled*, 2009
Cast polyurethane resin, stitched and dyed canvas, acrylic paint; 12.2 x 4.3 x 2.4 inches
Courtesy of the artist and The Modern Institute, Glasgow

Born in 1982 in New York (USA), **Meredith James** lives and works in New York. www.meredith-james.com

[p. 146–147] *Day Shift*, 2009
Installation: mixed media
Video: 3:12
Room: 80 x 80 x 47.5 inches
AP 1 of edition of 5 + 2 AP
Courtesy of the artist and Marc Jancou Contemporary, New York

Born in 1959 in Lakewood (California, USA), **Larry Johnson** lives and works in Los Angeles.

[p. 102–103] *Untitled (PIX PIX PIX PIX)*, 2010
Color photograph; framed: 35 x 70 inches
Edition of 3 + 2 AP
Courtesy of the artist and Marc Jancou Contemporary, New York

[p. 106] *Untitled (Cinema Moralia)*, 2010
Color photograph; framed: 50 x 48 inches
Edition 3 +2 APs
Courtesy of the artist and Marc Jancou Contemporary, New York

Born in 1978 in Warsaw (Poland), **Dorota Jurczak** lives and works in Brussels.

[p.128] *Introligator*, 2010
Pencil and ink on paper; 14.37 x 6.5 inches
Courtesy of the artist and Corvi-Mora, London

[p.129] *Lampa*, 2007
Mixed media; 10.2 x 9.4 x 5.9 inches
Courtesy of the artist and Corvi-Mora, London

Born in 1977 in Gainesville (Florida, USA), **Justin Lieberman** lives and works in New York.

[p. 58–59] *The Corrector's Custom Prefab House*, 2009
Mixed media; overall dimensions variable
Courtesy of the artist and Marc Jancou Contemporary, New York

[p. 130] *Either/Or*, 2010
Mixed media; framed: 85 x 52 x 2.75 inches
Courtesy Marc Jancou Contemporary, New York

Born in 1980 in San Jose (California, USA), **Nick Lowe** lives and works in Los Angeles.

[p. 104] *The Muppet Show*, 2009–2010
India ink on paper; 14 x 11 inches
Courtesy of the artist and Marc Jancou Contemporary, New York

[p. 105] *Text Face*, 2007–2010
Graphite on paper; framed:
15.75 x 12.75 inches
Courtesy of the artist and Marc
Jancou Contemporary, New York

Born in 1969 in Victoria (Australia),
David Noonan lives and works in
London.

[p. 94] *Untitled*, 2009
Silkscreen on jute and linen
collage; 60.6 x 43.3 inches
Courtesy of Foxy Production,
New York

[p. 95] *Untitled*, 2009
Silkscreen on jute and linen
collage; framed: 120 x 84.2 inches
Courtesy of the artist and Roslyn
Oxley Gallery, Sydney

[p. 96] *Untitled* (Orlando), 2010
Silkscreen on birch plywood, steel;
66.93 x 47.24 x 25.59 inches
Courtesy of the artist and Marc
Jancou Contemporary, New York

Born in 1978 in Los Angeles (USA),
Ry Rocklen lives and works in
Los Angeles.

[p. 136–137] *On the Fourth Day*,
2009
Mattress, aqua resin, tiles, grout;
43 x 36 x 11 inches
Courtesy of the artist and Marc
Jancou Contemporary, New York

[p. 138] *My Delorean 2*, 2010
Cage, screen, aqua resin,
fiberglass, mortar, mirror;
24 x 17 x 16 inches
Courtesy of the artist and Marc
Jancou Contemporary, New York

Born an American in 1972 in
Bitburg (Germany), **Sterling Ruby**
lives and works in Los Angeles.
www.sterlingrubystudio.com

[p. 72–73] *ACTS/KKDETHZ*, 2009
Formica, wood, spray paint,
and urethane; overall:
60.5 x 62.5 x 34 inches
Courtesy of the artist, Los Angeles

[p. 74] *Husbands/Sunburn P.O.P*,
2010
Fabric, fiber fill, zippers, Formica,
and wood; overall: 104 x 78 x 48
inches; alabaster pedestal:
24 x 78 x 48 inches
Courtesy of the artist; Xavier
Hufkens Gallery, Brussels;
and Marc Jancou Contemporary,
New York

Born in 1952 in Midland (Michigan,
USA), **Jim Shaw** lives and works in
Los Angeles.

[p. 84] *Blake/Boring*, 2010
Pencil and ink on paper; 12 x 9 inches
Courtesy of the artist; Galerie
Praz-Delavallade, Paris; and Marc
Jancou Contemporary, New York

[p. 85] *Blake/Boring*, 2010
Pencil and ink on paper; 12 x 9 inches
Courtesy of the artist and Patrick
Painter Inc., Santa Monica

[p. 86] *Dream Object ("A cartoon
figure had pendulous eyes on an
acetate overlay. Also there were
used condoms attached so I said
it would be perfect for an AIDS
benefit.")*, 2007
Ink, paint, and condoms on paper;
47.8 x 29.8 inches
Courtesy of Metro Pictures Gallery,
New York

Born in 1967 in Schwarzach
(Austria), **Torsten Slama** lives and
works in Brussels.

[p. 60] *SAPA Cement Plant*, 2008
Oil on canvas; 48.8 x 34.5 inches
Courtesy of Galerie Vera Gliem,
Cologne

[p. 61] *Cooperative Raiffeisen Institute Wilhelm Reich*, 2008
Oil on canvas; 35.5 x 67 inches
Courtesy of Galerie Vera Gliem, Cologne

Born in 1977 in Detroit (USA), **Michael E. Smith** lives and works in Detroit.

[p. 145] *Untitled*, 2009
Melted ink pens; 9 x 5 x 1 inches
Courtesy of the artist

Born in 1979 in Oxford (England), **Lucy Stein** lives and works in Berlin. www.pindalinda.com

[p. 126] *Everything Rhymes with Your Condition*, 2010
Ink and felt tip pen on paper;
9.84 x 13.78 inches
Courtesy of the artist and
Gimpel Fils, London

[p. 127] *Catherine Wheel*, 2009
Oil on canvas; 62.99 x 70.91 inches
Courtesy of the artist and
Gimpel Fils, London

Born in 1968 in Hamburg (Germany), **Stefan Thater** lives and works in Berlin.

[p. 114] *Keys*, 2008
Ink and turpentine on paper;
24 x 34 inches
Courtesy of the artist and
HOTEL, London

[p. 115] *Untitled*, 2005
Acrylic on board; 63 x 35 inches
Courtesy of the artist and Galerie
Daniel Buchholz, Cologne and
Berlin; Galerie Karin Guenther,
Hamburg; HOTEL, London

Born in 1982 in Paris (France), and raised in Texas, **Jacques Vidal** lives and works in Bridgeport, Connecticut.

[p. 70] *What-Else-Could-We-Do*, 2008
Chalkboard paint on wood;
17 x 10 x 7 inches
Courtesy of the artist and Marc
Jancou Contemporary, New York

[p. 71] *Guard Duty*, 2010
Watercolor on paper; unframed:
24 x 32 inches
Courtesy of the artist and Marc
Jancou Contemporary, New York

This book is published on the occasion of the exhibition *Rive gauche/Rive droite* organized in Paris in September 2010 in six different locations (Magasin Deyrolle, Lefebvre & Fils, Résidence de Jean-Marcel Camard, Galerie Catherine Houard, Saint Honoré Art Consulting, Espace Azzedine Alaia).

The publication has received generous support from:

Mauboussin, Paris
www.mauboussin.com
MAUBOUSSIN

Institut Le Rosey, Rolle
www.lerosey.ch
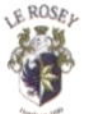

Château d'Esclans, Domaine
Sacha Lichine
www.chateaudesclans.com
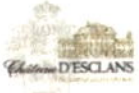

Domaine Pascal Jolivet
www.pascal-jolivet.com/
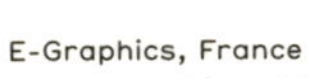
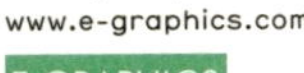

E-Graphics, France
www.e-graphics.com
E-GRAPHICS

L'Ecume des pages, Paris
www.ecumedespages.fr

Exhibit-E, New York
www.exhibit-e.com
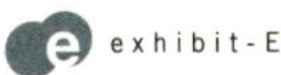

Icart, Paris
www.icartparis.com
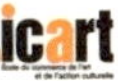

Magellan, Fine Art Services,
New York
www.magellanfas.com
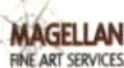

MBB
www.mbbsa.com

Fondation d'Entreprise Ricard
www.fondation-entreprise-ricard.com
FONDATION
D'ENTREPRISE
RICARD

Bordier & Cie
www.bordier.com
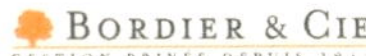

ACKNOWLEDGMENTS BY MARC JANCOU

First, I would like to sincerely thank the artists:
Michael Bauer, Alexandra Bircken, Cris Brodahl, Carter, Ross Chisholm, Michael Cline, Steven Claydon, Slawomir Elsner, Charlie Hammond, Andreas Hofer, Christian Holstad, Des Hughes, Richard Hughes, Meredith James, Larry Johnson, Dorota Jurczak, Justin Lieberman, Nick Lowe, David Noonan, Ry Rocklen, Sterling Ruby, Jim Shaw, Torsten Slama, Michael Smith, Lucy Stein, Stefan Thater, and Jacques Vidal.

As well as the following galleries and partners:
HOTEL: Margherita Hohenlohe, Darren Flook, and Christabel Stewart; Herald Street: Nicky Verber and Ash L'Ange; Xavier Hufkens: Xavier Hufkens, Simon Devolder, and Mathieu Paris; Salon 94: Jeanne Greenberg and David Fierman; IBID Projects: Magnus Edensvard and Tobias Wagner; Steven Claydon Studio: Oliver Robb; Sorcha Dallas; Hauser and Wirth: Julia Lenz; Metro Pictures: Allison Card and Manuela Mozo; Massimo de Carlo: Anna Maria Soverini; Ancient & Modern: Bruce Haines; Modern Institute: Toby Webster and Andrew Hamilton; Corvi-Mora: Tommaso Corvi-Mora and Tabitha Langton-Lockton; Sterling Ruby Studio: Natasha Garcia Lomas, Devon Oder, and Alexis Rose; Praz-Delavallade: René-Julien Praz, Bruno Delavallade, and Eléonore Lambertie; Jim Shaw Studio: Sachi Yoshimoto; Galerie Karin Guenther: Karin Guenther; Gimpel Fils: Jackie Haliday; Galerie Vera Gliem : Vera Gliem.

A warm and sincere thank you to the *Rive gauche/Rive droite* hosts:
Azzedine Alaia: Azzedine Alaia, Caroline Bazin, Morgane Denis, Sylvie Grumbach, and Mikaël-Khan Panni; Jean Marcel Camard; Saint Honoré Art Consulting: Marc Blondeau, Étienne Breton, and Clémence Dollier; Blondeau Fine Art Services: Marine Galley; Lefebvre & Fils Louis Lefebvre and Christiane Bricnet; Deyrolle: Louis Albert de Broglie, Pascale Nowicki, and Peio Rahola; Catherine Houard and Cécile Berger Brams.

As well as to the contributors of this book:
Lionel Bovier, Clément Dirié, and Gilles Gavillet at JRP|Ringier; Yves Aupetitallot and Alexis Jakubowicz for their texts.

I would also like to thank the following persons for their support and availability:
Bertille Achard de la Vente, Jacques Babando, Léonard Bénichou Weil, Henri Benkoski, Dominique Benoit, Sébastien Blondeau, Olivier Bouchara, Philippe Boulet, Pia de Brante, Gilbert Cadoche, Florence Camard, Isabelle Camard, Belen Canovas, Gérard Cirurel, Marie-Virginie Dru, Franck Gilardo, Charles Guyot, Joy Henderiks, Pamela Jancou, Aurélie Julien, Cyril Karaoglan, Didier et Clémence Krzentowski, Réjane Lacoste, Tim Lafon, Jean-Christophe Laizeau, Marie-France Lavarini, Jean-Pierre Lecoq, André Paulin, Marco et Françoise Pedrazzini, Didier Peronnin, Jean–Pierre Petit, Agnès Pinaire, Corentin Quideau, Philippe Rudloff, Sonia Rykiel, Mélita Toscan du Plantier, Xavier Samson, Valérie Solvit, Maxime Vibert et Denise Vilgrain.

My gratitude goes to the following
partners for their support of the
project:
Violante Avogardo di Vigliano,
Pierre Bergeaud, Christophe Burtin,
Charles Brunswick, Jean-François
Dubos, Catherine Gallion, Philippe
Gimond, Philippe Gudin, Meryll
Hermann, Sacha Lichine, Clément
Malochet, Billy Maker, Dan Miller,
Sam Mink, Julia and Stefan Muuls,
Alain Némarq, Laurent Plantier,
Lorraine Ricard, Serge Robert,
and Carole Siljegovic.

Last but not least, thanks to:
Kelly Woods and Kim Treanor
at Marc Jancou Contemporary,
New York; Laura Daniels, and
David Hadjer at the Paris office;
and to the interns Chloé Berne
Kergus, Titou Camard, Carole
Cossart, Marie Duffour, Audren
Husson, Charlotte Irondelle, Leila
de Lagausie, and Sara Tarter.

www.marcjancou.com

PUBLICATION

Exhibition Curator and Book Editor
Marc Jancou

Editorial Coordination
Clément Dirié and Kelly Woods

Translations
Susan Pickford for the texts by
Yves Aupetitallot, Alexis
Jakubowicz, and Marc Jancou

Design
Gavillet & Rust/Eigenheer, Geneva

Cover Image
Dorota Jurczak, *Untitled*, 2008
Ink, acrylic and oil on canvas,
24.8 x 19.75 inches
Courtesy of the artist and
Corvi-Mora, London

Photo Credits
Guy Archard (p. 94, 95); Andy Keate
(p. 37, 44); LeeAnn Nickel
(p. 84, 85); Robert Wedemeyer
(p. 72–73, 74); Cary Whittier (p. 55,
56, 57, 58–59, 70, 71, 102–103,
104, 105, 106, 112, 113, 136–137,
138, 146–147)

Production
Musumeci S.P.A., Quart (Aosta)

Typeface
Hermes-Sans (www.optimo.ch)

Published by

JRP|Ringier
Letzigraben 134
CH–8047 Zurich
T +41 (0) 43 311 27 50
F +41 (0) 43 311 27 51
E info@jrp-ringier.com
www.jrp-ringier.com

ISBN 978-3-03764-154-5
(French edition available:
ISBN 978-3-03764-155-2)

Produced in Europe

JRP|Ringier books are available
internationally at selected book-
stores and from the following
distribution partners:

Switzerland
Buch 2000, AVA Verlagsauslieferung
AG, Centralweg 16, CH–8910
Affoltern a.A., buch2000@ava.ch,
www.ava.ch

France
Les Presses du réel, 35 rue Colson,
F–21000 Dijon,
info@lespressesdureel.com,
www.lespressesdureel.com

Germany and Austria
Vice Versa Vertrieb,
Immanuelkirchstrasse 12, D–10405
Berlin, info@vice-versa-vertrieb.de,
www.vice-versa-vertrieb.de

UK and other European countries
Cornerhouse Publications, 70
Oxford Street, UK–Manchester M1
5NH, publications@cornerhouse.org,
www.cornerhouse.org/books

USA, Canada, Asia, and Australia
D.A.P./Distributed Art Publishers,
155 Sixth Avenue, 2nd Floor,
USA–New York, NY 10013,
dap@dapinc.com, www.artbook.com

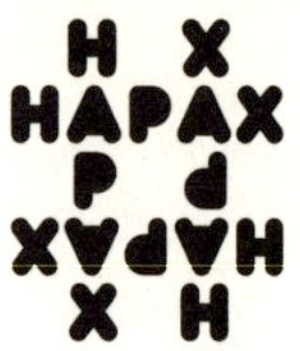

In the same series:

MALCOLM MCLAREN
Musical Paintings (2009)
English edition
ISBN 978-3-03764-058-6

SCOTT KING
Anxiety & Depression (2008)
English edition
ISBN 978-3-905829-69-3